Basic Guidelines For Christian Dating

Maverick .N Frost

Introduction

This book is a delightful journey for couples seeking to strengthen their bond while embracing their faith. The guide is organized into various sections, each offering unique ideas and experiences for couples to enjoy together.

The guide opens with "Just the Two of Us," encouraging couples to cherish the simplicity of spending quality time together. It highlights the importance of nurturing the connection between partners through intimate moments and meaningful conversations.

The "Homegrown" section celebrates the joys of creating and cultivating a shared life. It suggests activities that allow couples to bond over shared projects, whether it's gardening, cooking, or DIY home improvements. This section promotes the idea that nurturing a life together can be a fulfilling adventure in itself.

"Creative & Culinary" takes couples on a culinary journey, emphasizing the pleasure of cooking and creating delicious meals together. It suggests exploring new recipes, hosting themed dinner nights, and nurturing the art of preparing food as a couple.

For couples who appreciate the great outdoors, "Outdoors & Adventure" offers a range of exciting activities to choose from. Whether it's hiking, camping, or embarking on nature adventures, this section encourages couples to connect with each other and with the beauty of the natural world.

"Together in Service" promotes the idea of giving back as a couple. It provides suggestions for engaging in acts of kindness and volunteering together, reinforcing the values of compassion and service that are central to many Christian beliefs.

"Group Dates" introduces the concept of shared experiences with friends and other couples. It encourages couples to socialize, build connections, and enjoy fun activities in the company of others, fostering a sense of community.

The guide concludes with "Holidays & Special Occasions," offering ideas for celebrating significant moments and holidays as a couple. It suggests ways to infuse Christian values into holiday traditions and special occasions, emphasizing the importance of faith in these moments.

Throughout the guide, the focus remains on fostering a deep and meaningful connection between couples while staying true to their Christian beliefs. It encourages couples to embark on adventures together, whether they are small, everyday moments or grand, exciting experiences, all while strengthening their faith and commitment to each other.

Contents

CHAPTER ONE
Just the Two of Us

The dates in this chapter are centered on creating (or re-creating) moments that will ignite (or reignite) the romance. Staying attracted to your date is critical for sustaining the relationship over many seasons. The phrase "fall in love all over again" is something you should aim for throughout your relationship, not just during its early phases.

Of course, it's much easier to tap into the romance when you initially start to date. Everything is new, fresh, and exciting. Over time, however, it can become a bit of a challenge. Comfort levels set in. Jobs, kids, and life take over. Before you know it, you are repeating the same dates over and over simply because "it's what we do." You may start to think you know each other too well to seek new adventures. Don't allow this mindset to set in!

This chapter will pull you out of your comfort zone and explore date ideas that will keep things exciting. These particular dates are special because they're designed to bring you closer to your date mentally, emotionally, and spiritually. And if you've reached that part of your relationship, most of these dates should draw you closer together physically, as well.

Are you ready to fall in love (all over again)? Let's dive into how you can bring those butterflies back to life.

SOCIAL MEDIA MANIA

Jesus called out to them, "Come, follow me, and I will show you how to fish for people!"

—Mark 1:17

Create one new post on every social media platform you and your date use. Use these sites to send out a message that promotes love—for yourself, for each other, or for God. Make sure each post fits each platform; do not just take one picture and post it everywhere. Make each post unique and engaging.

What's the Word?

Nowadays, nearly everyone is using social media to share their thoughts, opinions, agendas, and more. One of the major aspects of social media, of course, is who you follow or who follows you based on your connection and what you post. Jesus understood the value of followers better than anyone else. In Mark 1:17, He mentions how His followers would not only be impacted personally but could also influence others. Be mindful of what you post and share with the world. Your thoughts, opinions, faith, and even your relationship can be used to uplift, support, and inspire others. More important, take note of who you follow and understand why others are following you. Not only will it impact you personally, but it could also impact your relationship.

Good For

- Communication
- Playfulness
- Being present

Tip

- Agree on which social platforms you and your date will decide to post. If you are planning to do a challenge or dance trend, select it before your date so you can practice your moves.
- Before the date, share posts and videos you like as a way to connect with each other leading up to the date.
- Have ready all the props and outfits you need to create your posts.
- Be positive and encouraging in your captions and hashtags. What you post will represent you both.

- It's not about the likes! This date is about creating something as a couple that is uplifting and that reflects your personalities. If you both like it, that's all that matters.

LEVEL UP

Clean up your social media and remove the accounts you no longer desire to follow. As a couple, follow a few new accounts that might encourage you to exercise healthy relationship habits!

Talking Points

- What is your favorite social media platform and why?
- What inspires you to post something?
- What makes you like a post or follow someone?
- How do you look to social media to build/inspire your faith?
- How do you look to social media to build/inspire this relationship?
- What are some ways you can use your platform to share uplifting/encouraging posts with your followers?
- What are some negative or toxic aspects of social media you should watch out for?

WHEN WE WERE YOUNG

When I was a child, I spoke and thought and reasoned as a child. But when I grew up, I put away childish things.

—1 Corinthians 13:11

Go back to your childhood and create a date using some of your most favorite memories. Plan a day to go visit a playground, an arcade, or a trampoline center; watch your favorite childhood movie; play your favorite game; or listen to your favorite childhood songs. Be sure to sprinkle some of your favorite childhood candies, drinks, and other nostalgic foods into your date.

What's the Word?

As a child, you did things differently than as an adult. Although you are now mature enough to know that childish behavior doesn't take you very far, some things from your childhood are worth cherishing. Your creativity. Your energy. Your courage. Your faith. Each is a great attribute to carry into your adult life and relationships. On the contrary, temper tantrums, selfishness, and impatience are qualities you should look to overcome as an adult. Rather than carrying these negative traits into your adulthood and relationship, circle back to the lessons God has taught you along the way that could step up your faith and produce a maturity that can withstand the seasons to come. If there is anything you should take away from this date, it's that some childhood things are worth keeping, and others are long overdue to be left behind.

Good For

- Playfulness
- Vulnerability
- Honoring Values

Tip

- You can combine your past experiences to create one epic date or split your childhood favorites into two amazing blasts from the past.

- Remember that not everyone experienced a good childhood. Be mindful of the memories you share and be open and lend a listening ear if the conversation gets deep.
- Ask your parents or siblings what you were like as a child to help you recall some of your fondest childhood memories.
- Share old photos of yourself to bring up even more memories while creating unique conversations.
- It's okay to play! Let yourself step out of your adult comfort zone and enjoy feeling like a kid again.

LEVEL UP

Put on something for the date that you wore as a kid. It could be barrettes in your hair, glitter nail polish, or your favorite sports jersey.

Talking Points

- What was your favorite childhood memory? why did you love it so much?
- Do you remember God being a part of your childhood? If so, how?
- What are some ways your childhood has impacted this relationship?
- If there was one thing from your childhood that this date reminded you of (such as a tradition you once followed, or a song, activity, or food that used to make you happy), what would it be?

LET THERE BE LIGHT

Then God said, "Let there be light," and there was light.

—Genesis 1:3

Rise up bright and early to spend an entire morning together. Your date will begin at the crack of dawn (literally!) with you watching the sunrise together. Afterward, enjoy a lovely brunch, either at home or at a local diner. Cap off this morning date with a movie matinee.

What's the Word?

In the beginning, God created all things. He spoke the light into existence when He declared "Let there be light" in Genesis 1:3. Speaking life into something (or someone) is powerful. How often have you been doing so with your date and within this relationship? Could you be doing it more? To make the most of this relationship, try to form a new habit by speaking loving words frequently during your date. You can also create some positive affirmations for the relationship and share them with your partner. They can be as simple as letting your partner know they have a particular skill, or going deeper and sharing the specific potential you see in them.

Good For

- Intimacy
- Being present
- Affection
- Romance

Tip

- Be sure to check exactly when the sunrise will be so you don't oversleep. It might also be a good idea to scope out where to go to watch the sunrise so you don't miss the best part of the morning.
- As you watch the sunrise, bring your favorite morning beverage and a blanket in case it's chilly outside. You may want to wear comfortable clothing, too.
- Brunch is usually an inexpensive meal, but feel free to jazz it up a bit if you decide to make it at home. Add some fruit toppings to your pancakes, create an avocado bar with bacon and tomatoes, or squeeze some fresh orange juice. You can also create a playlist with some of your favorite songs.
- Throughout the date, continue to compliment your partner and speak affirmingly about your relationship and this morning you're sharing with them.
- This date is jam-packed and early, so be sure to get enough sleep the night before!

LEVEL UP

Take this date back to the beginning by remembering parts of your first date (what you said, special gifts, memorable songs) and incorporating them into this one.

Talking Points

- "In the beginning, God created . . ." What are some things God is currently creating in your season now, both in your individual lives and in this relationship?
- Would you like to set any new goals in this new season? If so, what?

- If you have had rough patches in this relationship in the past, what are some ways you can create and establish a "new beginning" to do better moving forward?

COUNT THE STARS

He counts the stars and calls them all by name.

—Psalm 147:4

Unlike the previous date, where everything took place at dawn, this date occurs at the very end of the day. Watch the sunset together over an evening picnic. As the sky gets darker and turns into night, spend some time gazing at the stars together.

What's the Word?

God designed each of us in a unique and creative way. We are not like anyone else in the world. Your relationship, therefore, like each constellation, is unique as well. Be confident in what God has joined in you and your date. You were brought together for a unique reason. Your strengths may complement your date's weaknesses. What you enjoy may shed a new light onto your date's life, which can cause them to grow for the better. Together, you may become a life-changing team that affects many. For better or worse, what you experience in this relationship will be unmatched; your life together will deliver valuable gifts and lessons that God intended just for you.

Good For

- Intimacy
- Being present
- Affection

- Romance

Tip

- Be sure to note the timing of the sunset and dress appropriately, as it can get cooler as the sun begins to set.
- In order to see the stars, you have to get away from bright lights. If you can, plan this date to take place in an open field or somewhere away from a city setting.
- Depending on the season, you may need to be mindful of nighttime bugs, such as mosquitos. Pack a citronella candle or some spray to keep the pests at bay.
- Check the forecast and plan to have this date on a clear night. The last thing you want to do is try to stargaze in the rain!
- If you cannot go outdoors in an open setting that will allow you to stargaze, create the scene indoors using glow-in-the-dark stars, a screensaver with a starlit setting, or some white Christmas lights you can hang from your ceiling.

LEVEL UP

Visit a planetarium to learn more about the stars and how truly unique they are.

Talking Points

- Each star, like each person, is unique to God. What are some unique things about your date that you love?
- What makes your date stand out from all the other people you could've dated?
- What about this particular relationship distinguishes it from your past relationships?

- How does knowing you are as unique as the stars to God make you feel?

SURPRISE, SURPRISE

"For I know the plans I have for you," says the Lord. "They are plans for good and not for disaster, to give you a future and a hope."

—Jeremiah 29:11

In this date, you will be calling all the shots for your date, and vice versa. You will select what your date will wear, what foods they will eat, and what activities they'll engage in. Your date will do the same for you. Although you can predict what you think your date would prefer in these categories, the fun part is you can switch it up and they have to go along with it!

What's the Word?

It's important to set goals, make plans, and take action. Ultimately, however, it's God's call as to what happens and what doesn't. The same applies to this relationship. You have to be okay with trusting in God, whether He takes your relationship to the next level or ends it before it reaches that point. Sure, it may not be the result you are going after, or you might face some challenging seasons in order to make your relationship stronger, but God's way is always meant for better, not worse, even if it doesn't seem that way. If you trust in God and His plans, you have to trust His will for this relationship. His plans are to give you a future and give you hope, so have faith, and trust in Him and in each other.

Good For

- Trust
- Playfulness
- Respect

Tip

- Resolve to respect and honor your partner. This date is not about humiliating them or making them do something just for your own pleasure. Remember, whatever you make them do, they can do right back to you! It's a good time to remember the Golden Rule.
- Get creative! Aside from their outfit and food options, you can choose which song your date will sing at karaoke, which movie they'll watch, which song they'll dance to, or in which video game you'll challenge them.
- This date could be a great way to pull each other out of your respective comfort zones. You never know what you might end up enjoying.
- This date ultimately requires a lot of trust, so treat it with caution. The last thing you want to do is break that trust. You want your date to feel safe with you, even if they're being challenged to try something new.

LEVEL UP

If you know your date has been wanting to do something, now is a good opportunity to nudge them in that direction.

Talking Points

- How much do you trust in God when it comes to directing your path and plans?

- Is there anything that keeps you from trusting God with this relationship?
- What can you and your partner do to build up your trust in each other?
- What surprised you about your partner's choices? Did you enjoy something new?

DANCE MODE

Praise His name with dancing, accompanied by tambourine and harp.

—Psalm 149:3

This date is all about dancing! If you're into dancing, you can go out to dance or learn a new dance together. If dancing is not your thing, you can take dance classes with your date (there are great tutorials on YouTube), or go to a dance club for the very first time. At the very least, set up a playlist of your favorite songs and dance the night away!

What's the Word?

Dancing allows your body to move freely and can be a great way to express yourself. Dancing for God is a liberating way to express your praise for Him. If you feel enough joy within yourself to move through dance, something must be going right in your relationship! Likewise, whenever you feel like praising God for all He is doing in you and your relationship, do not shy away from dancing your worship to Him!

Good For

* Playfulness
* Vulnerability
* Trust

Tip

* Not everyone is comfortable with dancing. Although it can be fun to step out of your comfort zone, don't make this experience unbearable for yourself or your date. And remember that not everyone is capable of dancing on their feet because of mobility issues. Meet your date where they are. Clapping, foot tapping and head bobbing can also help you feel the groove.
* Have fun dancing to different musical genres. Don't settle for just one style of dance; switch things up.
* Some dances are meant to make you move, and others can draw you close to each other. It's okay to get romantic and swoon over your date.
* Ever hear of praise dance? It's when a person (or a group of people) dance as a way to worship God. Look up some praise dances on YouTube and give it a go.
* Select a song you both love and try creating a dance together. Try not to feel self-conscious—just have fun!

LEVEL UP

If you're feeling especially brave, record a video of a dance you create with your date and upload it to your favorite social media site to share with others.

Talking Points

- What makes you feel like dancing?
- What keeps you from dancing?
- What comes to mind when you think of "praise dance," or dancing for the Lord?
- Does this relationship make you want to dance? Why or why not?

ALL THINGS NEW

But forget all that—it is nothing compared to what I am going to do. For I am about to do something new. See, I have already begun! Do you not see it? I will make a pathway through the wilderness. I will create rivers in the dry wasteland.

—Isaiah 43:18–19

In this date, you will be turning another person's junk into your treasure! Assign a dollar amount for you and your date ($15 to $40 each should be plenty). Visit your local thrift store or a local garage or yard sale in your neighborhood, and select clothes and accessories for your date. Whatever you are able to find for each other, you and your date must wear for the remainder of the date.

What's the Word?

God can take anything that is worn or old and make it new again, including your heart, your relationship, and your current season. You have to give God the space to do new things in your life, though. God has used some parts of your past relationships to reshape you, and you are using those lessons in this relationship. Likewise, parts of you are being renewed with every season. Do not feel weary when God takes something from your past and redesigns it into something totally different. Trust that no matter what "junk" God works with, it will always result in treasure.

Good For

- Trust
- Vulnerability
- Unconditional love

Tip

- If you've never shopped at a thrift store or a garage or yard sale, know that a little can go a long way. Having $30 is more than enough; even spending just $5 will get you something interesting!
- Allow enough time to shop for the right size and style for your date. Don't rush through the date. You can make a day of it and visit multiple shops or sales in your area.
- You may want to break this date up into two dates. The first date involves shopping for each other. On the second date, you and your date wear the items you purchased.
- Your outfits may not match. They may feel outdated. You might feel like you look silly. Use your flair and style to make it work! Add your accessories or pair the outfit with something you own.
- If this outfit is one-and-done, you can always donate it back to a thrift store after your date—along with some other items in your closet that you no longer wear.

LEVEL UP

Combine this date with another date, like "Let There Be Light" or "Count the Stars", and buy your entire picnic setting from the thrift store.

Talking Points

- Is there any part of your life where you see God making something new?
- Are there any new qualities in this relationship that you have never experienced in past relationships?
- How can you be a better partner in this relationship than in your past relationships?
- Did you see anything in the thrift store that intrigued you? What was it?

CONSIDER THE LILIES

And why worry about your clothing? Look at the lilies of the field and how they grow. They don't work or make their clothing, yet Solomon in all his glory was not dressed as beautifully as they are.

—Matthew 6:28–29

Nothing says romance better than flowers! On this date, visit a local florist. Examine the different flowers displayed: Take in their unique fragrance, note the filler flowers, and study how the various kinds of flowers come together to create marvelous bouquets. Then work together to create your version of the best, most romantic arrangement you've ever seen!

What's the Word?

God does not make junk. He pays very close attention to detail. God has considered every single aspect of this relationship. Don't believe me? Look at all the vast arrays of flowers you just encountered. Reflect on their fragrance, their design, and the wonderful feelings they evoke. Don't worry so much about this relationship. Whatever God is doing in it will be beautifully and carefully designed.

Good For

- Romance
- Affection
- Unconditional love

Tip

- Some rare flowers can be pricey. Be sure to set a budget and stick to it. No matter how little you have, you can find something stunning!
- If you don't want to keep the arrangement, consider creating the bouquet for someone who has played a supporting role in your relationship.
- If there is no florist nearby, check out a local grocery store and purchase different bouquets you can use to create your own.
- For a gift that keeps on giving, consider buying flower seeds and growing your own beautiful bunch over the course of the season.
- Ditch the flower shop altogether and spend a day outdoors collecting wildflowers.

LEVEL UP

Pair your bouquet excursion with a trip to your local greenhouse or botanical garden to get an even fuller experience of the unique flowers God has created for us to enjoy.

Talking Points

- What's your favorite flower? Why?
- In what ways have flowers played a role in your relationship?
- How can flowers be used to symbolize your love for your date?
- In what ways can you incorporate more flowers (and what they symbolize) into your relationship?
- What makes your relationship beautiful?
- What worries are distracting you from appreciating the beautiful blessings in your life?

DREAM DESTINATION

But they were looking for a better place, a heavenly homeland. That is why God is not ashamed to be called their God, for He has prepared a city for them.

—Hebrews 11:16

Select a dream destination. It could be a city like Paris, a country like China, or even a fantasy place from your favorite movie, like Willy Wonka's chocolate factory. Design a date that captures the tastes, sounds, culture, and themes from this place. The location and details are up to you!

What's the Word?

Whether you're able to travel someday or just imagining for fun, setting your sights on far-off destinations can make you feel excited and hopeful. Sharing your dreams and having your date alongside you to dream with is the cherry on top of that amazing blessing. Looking forward to a dream destination is undoubtedly exciting, but remember where the ultimate dream destination is. While you are still here on Earth, enjoying this moment and dreaming of visiting one of God's beautiful places, keep in mind there is another destination that far surpasses any place you and your date can imagine: heaven.

Good For

- Encouraging each other
- Affection
- Support

Tip

- Take turns selecting where you'd like to go so each person can explore their own unique dream destination. You can even turn this into two dates, one for each of you.
- Go all in. Learn a couple of phrases (or songs) that are connected to this place. Research the type of music that is popular there and the foods it is particularly known for.
- Research will become your best friend for this date. Pick the destination in advance and give yourself plenty of time to collect all you need to execute the perfect date.
- If you're married, consider re-creating your honeymoon destination, or use this date as a way to spark plans of a potential second honeymoon.
- If your destination is outside of the English-speaking realm, set the mood by streaming a movie in that language.

LEVEL UP

For this date, wear an outfit that pays tribute to the destination you're dreaming of.

Talking Points

- why do you wish to travel to this particular place?
- what was the best trip you've ever been on?
- If you went on a trip with your date, what is one thing you should know about them? what is one thing they should know about you?
- Heaven can be considered the ultimate "dream destination." what do you imagine it will look and feel like?

SECOND CHANCE

Make allowance for each other's faults, and forgive anyone who offends you. Remember, the Lord forgave you, so you must forgive others.

—Colossians 3:13

Re-create a date during which something went terribly wrong between you and your date. Repeat every single step that led up to the mishap, but this time make things right, such as taking a different action or rephrasing something you said. whatever you wish you could've done then, do it now.

What's the Word?

No matter what you do, God is willing and ready to forgive us and restore us. Every time. If God can forgive all our faults and failings, we should be able to practice the same principles toward the people we love. Although it might not be easy, it's essential if you wish to see your relationship grow and stay strong over time. Trying to love and learn from each other with offense or hurt in your heart leads to the beginning of the end. The best thing you can do for your relationship is forgive and allow the opportunity to try to love again.

Good For

- Trust
- communication
- compassion
- vulnerability
- Unconditional love

Tip

- Make sure both of you are comfortable conducting this date so you can avoid any triggers of pain, trauma, or wounds that have yet to heal.
- Write out what you felt during the first date and what you wish would've happened. Read the note during the second date.
- This date requires a large dose of humility in order to admit to faults and face embarrassing moments. Be prepared.
- This date may require some very mature conversations about very real feelings. Be ready to L.U.V. (Listen, Understand, Validate).
- The goal of this date is to rectify a moment in your relationship that took a wrong turn. Both parties must be willing to work toward a resolution.

LEVEL UP

While redoing this date and trying to create a better ending, use your partner's love language to emphasize and speak love to them. If your partner is doing the same for you, be sure to show appreciation and gratitude. See the Resources section for tools on how to learn your love language.

Talking Points

- Are you willing to forgive your date for offending, embarrassing, or hurting you?
- How did you feel going into this second-chance date?
- How did you feel after redoing the date?
- Moving forward, how can you both make the most out of unfortunate moments like the earlier date?
- What have you learned about your date (and yourself) after experiencing this date and giving each other a second chance?

CHAPTER TWO

Homegrown

If you're anything like me, a simple night in often sounds way better than a fun-filled night out. Going out for dates has its perks, but it can also be quite draining! Who knew that having so much fun could leave you feeling exhausted? Homegrown DIY dates are a safe choice that keeps your budget low and your comfort levels high. For parents, it's probably the best way to make the most of your alone time once the kiddos are asleep. And if you're an introvert, the at-home date might be your favorite.

If you're not careful, however, those at-home dates can start to feel a bit like the movie Groundhog Day—a never-ending cycle of the same old activities that generate low enthusiasm between you and your date. Although staying at home for dates may seem easier, it often leads to a dull dating life. You have to stay motivated to keep dating fun!

Whether you're unable to leave your home or you want to "just chill," there are some great ways to get creative and grow your relationship through dating. The scenery may be the same for each date, but the imagination and creativity is not. In order to take any of these at-home dates to the next level, you have to be ready and willing to think outside the box and focus on what really matters: you, your date, and growing together.

WISH YOU WERE HERE

Kind words are like honey—sweet to the soul and healthy for the body.

—Proverbs 16:24

On this date, buy some postcards and write kind words to your favorite friends and family members. Tell them all the things you appreciate about them and, if applicable, the positive ways they've influenced or supported your relationship. If they live too far away to visit regularly, catch them up on some awesome things you and your partner have done together. Afterward, write a special letter to your date that you'll send sometime later.

What's the Word?

compliments and nice words feel great. God wants us to speak in love and share that love with others. What better way to express love than to pour it out through kind words? Words that encourage, edify, and uplift can pull anyone out of a bad mood. As you write to those you love, consider how often you share kind words with your date. Just imagine what more nurturing words could do for their mind, body, and spirit—and for your entire relationship.

Good For

- communication
- Honoring values
- Being present

Tip

- Be sure you have everything you need to mail off your postcards, like stamps, cards, and addresses.
- Decide on the number of postcards each of you will write out—you don't want to make your list so long that the date feels overwhelming! Between 5 and 10 postcards each is a good range.
- Although postcards are fun, fast, and easy, you can always send greeting cards or simple handwritten letters instead.
- Do not skip writing a letter to your date! If you don't do it now, you won't do it. The goal is for them to have your kind words on hand when they need them most.

- Be sure to take breaks from writing to enjoy your partner—get up and stretch, grab snacks, and engage with each other.

LEVEL UP

Make your own postcards using pictures of yourself and incorporating graphic designs. You can create cards using the photo center at a local pharmacy, or you can use an online graphic site like Canva.

Talking Points

- Why are the people you are sending postcards to important to you?
- What kind of relationship do you currently have with these people?
- Are these people aware of your current relationship? If not, why?
- What is the best way to encourage you whenever you feel down?

BOARD GAMES WITH A TWIST

If you love me, obey my commandments.

—John 14:15

Collect board games or a deck of cards to play a series of games on your date. As you follow the rules for each game, add your own rule that your date must follow. For example, maybe the loser must refill all snacks and beverages for the rest of the night, or whoever rolls a five must give the other a five-minute foot rub.

What's the Word?

Rules are meant to protect us and keep order. Parents setting rules for their kids understand this concept; children who must follow the rules may not. God created rules for this very reason—to protect and keep order within our lives. As in your relationship with God, there are rules within your romantic relationship, which you may not have discussed, that are meant to build you up rather than keep you down. Respect the rules of this game and you'll win every time.

Good For

- Respect and boundaries
- Friendship
- Intimacy
- Playfulness

Tip

- Make sure both parties agree to the rules before setting them. You don't want anyone to feel uncomfortable and disengage from the date altogether. Remember, these dates are meant to draw you and your date together, not to humiliate or disrespect anyone.
- If you're married, you can totally steam up this date by creating some spicy rules that involve your clothes, kissing, massages, and more.
- Keep the rules fun, simple, and fair. Each of you should have a chance to win and the opportunity to make some rules.
- If you have only one game to play, add your personal rules after every round.

- Let your competitive side out, but don't go overboard (pun intended) with your winning attitude. Remember, they are only games—there is no need for sore losers.

LEVEL UP
Create an ultimate prize or trophy that the person who won the most games receives at the end of the night.

Talking Points

- What have been your biggest wins in life? Your biggest losses?
- How do you feel about God's rules (His commandments)?
- How do you currently honor God's rules in your life?
- What are the rules within your relationship?
- What happens if someone breaks one of the relationship rules?
- What happens when you and your date both honor your relationship rules?

CASTING VISION (BOARD)

Then the Lord said to me, "Write my answer plainly on tablets, so that a runner can carry the correct message to others. This vision is for a future time. It describes the end, and it will be fulfilled. If it seems slow in coming, wait patiently, for it will surely take place. It will not be delayed."

—Habakkuk 2:2–3

Gather old magazines, quotes, words, Bible verses, pictures, drawings, or other scraps to help you create a vision board that reflects your goals, dreams, and faith. You will then spend time together creating your own board. When you're done, review the boards, sharing your dreams and visions. Pray over each other and your vision boards together.

What's the Word?

God is the biggest planner of all. When He reveals some of those plans through our dreams and desires, we should be reminded of them often. Seeing a visual reminder of your dreams on your vision board will not only encourage you on a consistent basis but also remind you that God has placed some amazing dreams within your heart. The same can be said about your relationship. God has planned for some amazing goals and dreams for you and your date to experience together. Stay focused on those visions and not on what aims to destroy them or distract you from reaching them.

Good For

- Encouraging each other
- Honoring values
- Communication
- Support

Tip

- Leave nothing off of your vision board, and don't be afraid to dream big. Put down anything and everything your heart craves for yourself and your life.

- Your vision board can include inspiring phrases, words, locations, names, and even small materials, such as fabrics, flowers, and receipts. Add whatever you need in order to express your vision. There is no one way to do this.
- Collect your materials beforehand (such as old magazines, glue sticks, scissors, or markers) so you're not scrambling to find these items during your date.
- Hang your vision board where you can see it often.
- As you and your partner work on your dream boards, be sure to encourage them in their dreams and be curious enough to ask for more details. Support goes a long way when your date dreams big.

LEVEL UP

Together with your date, create a vision board for your relationship. Incorporate all the dreams and visions you have for your union.

Talking Points

- What visions do you have for yourself?
- What visions do you have for this relationship?
- Has God ever given you a vision for your life? What was it?
- Which dream or vision scares you most?
- How can you and your partner best support each other in your dreams and visions?

YOU COOK, I LISTEN

But Jesus told him, "No! The Scriptures say, 'People do not live by bread alone, but by every word that comes from the mouth of God.'"

—Matthew 4:4

select a meal that you and your partner can both make that requires multiple courses (such as salad, soup, main dish, sides, dessert). Take turns cooking the courses of the meal. while one person is cooking, the other must select their favorite songs to listen to. when the person cooking is done with their portion of the meal, switch roles.

What's the Word?

You can learn a lot from what you listen to. Likewise, you can learn a lot from what someone cooks and how they cook it. And although enjoying a lovely meal together with your date is great, the most fulfilling aspect of this date should be listening to and getting to know each other on a deeper level. It's the same way with God. Although His provisions are great, listening to Him through His word, biblical teachings, church sermons, and even worship music is what will fill you most.

Good For

- Encouraging each other
- Teamwork
- Honesty
- support

Tip

- choose a meal that is easy to cook and to divide between the two of you.

- Be open and secure in the music you select. Let it reflect you and your musical taste! Don't be afraid to be yourself.
- You are meant to take turns cooking and acting as DJ. It can be easy to get distracted, however, if you enjoy one role more than the other. If it helps, set a timer to go off at regular intervals in order to continue switching throughout the date.
- You can get music anywhere. If you need help finding a particular song, go to apps like Spotify or even YouTube to find it.
- Once you're ready to eat, select a playlist you can both listen to. It's especially helpful to choose instrumental-only songs so you can focus on connecting with each other during this portion of the date.

LEVEL UP

Create a playlist of your favorite songs from this date to play throughout your relationship. As your relationship progresses, add some new songs you both enjoy that remind you of your love for each other.

Talking Points

- Do any of the songs you selected have a personal story behind them? If so, what is it?
- What did you learn about your date based on their song selection?
- Who's the better cook? Why?
- Who's the better DJ? Why?
- Although this date may have seemed fairly simple to execute, were there any special moments that stood out to you?

BARISTA BAR

I thirst for God, the living God. When can I go and stand before Him?

—Psalm 42:2

Re-create your favorite coffee shop. Serve teas, specialty coffees, and even a few pastries. Choose a room in your home to act as the coffeehouse and decorate the space with plants, throw pillows, and anything else that creates the right atmosphere. Complete the scene with a very chill coffeehouse playlist.

What's the Word?

When the alarm goes off and it's time to get your day going, the first thing on your mind is usually a nice cup of coffee. In fact, for many of us, coffee becomes the solution just about any time we feel the need for a pick-me-up. Coffee is great, but when you put it into perspective, you should really be focused on God to lift you up and get you energized for the day. In the same manner that you are seeking coffee to jump-start your tired spirit, are you also looking to God to give you strength in those weary moments?

Good For

- Communication
- Being present
- Friendship

Tip

- You can look up specialty coffee recipes online or even ask your local coffee shop.

- To set the scene, be sure to clean up a space where you can actually sit and enjoy your coffee time. Dim the lights, play some music, and set the tone for a quiet and relaxing vibe.
- If you'd like, you can create a coffee bar with all the ingredients so you and your date can explore all your barista beverage options.
- Setting a coffeehouse atmosphere requires you to disconnect from the outside world. Turn off the TV and try to disconnect from your electronic devices as much as possible.
- Searching for specialty coffee items may require you to shop online or at health food stores. Remember that common household staples, such as vanilla extract, cinnamon, or chocolate, can also go a long way!

LEVEL UP

Create a specialty coffee drink at home together, give it a name, and order it next time you visit a coffee shop.

Talking Points

- Discuss your favorite coffeehouse beverage. Why is it your favorite?
- Do you need your cup of joe in the morning? Why or why not?
- What impact does coffee/caffeine have on your life?
- How does your dependence on coffee to feel energized relate to your relationship to God?

LET IT GROW

It's not important who does the planting, or who does the watering. What's important is that God makes the seed grow.

—1 Corinthians 3:7

Plants improve the quality of any living environment. Spend a day together caring for your houseplants. Repot the ones that have grown and require more space. Prune the dead leaves and flowers. Fertilize them to provide an extra dose of love and nutrients. If you don't have a plant in your house, this date is the perfect time to choose one together. If you prefer to enjoy your plants outdoors, use this date to start a garden.

What's the Word?

As the Bible states, although we all can do what is needed in order to grow something, God is the ultimate factor in determining whether it actually grows. The same can be said about your relationship. Even though you should continue to do whatever you can to grow the relationship and learn to love each other, giving this area of your life to God to take care of requires trust and faith in God Himself. No matter how much you invest in and care for it, it is up to God to allow you and your date to flourish together. Does it make you worried? Or does it make you trust God more?

Good For

- Compassion
- Affection
- Teamwork
- Unconditional love

Tip

* Not all plants are equal. For example, a cactus requires minimal care, whereas a delicate orchid requires a lot of attention. If you are looking to get a new plant during this date, consider its requirements before purchasing.
* Planting can get a bit messy, so be sure you are wearing clothes you don't mind getting dirty.
* Learn more about caring for your specific plants by consulting a plant book or doing research online.
* You might not have a green thumb. Your focus shouldn't be on perfection, but on doing your part to care for something.
* Not every plant thrives and flourishes. Do not feel like a failure if your plants don't make it. The time you spent together with your date produces the ultimate growth you're looking for.

LEVEL UP

Start a new plant from a seed or seedling and watch it grow throughout your relationship. You can keep it in your home or plant it outdoors in hopes that it will thrive in that outdoor air and warm sun.

Talking Points

* What has been your experience growing plants? If your family had a garden growing up, describe it.
* What do you think a houseplant can bring to a home?
* How does caring for your plants help you reflect on God's care for us?
* In what ways have you grown as an individual since the start of the relationship?
* In what ways do you see your relationship growing?

- What areas of this relationship need watering? Pruning?

SPA-LA-LA

Then Jesus said, "Come to me, all of you who are weary and carry heavy burdens, and I will give you rest."

—Matthew 11:28

Make a spa day at home for you and your date to enjoy. Create stations in your home for facials, mani-pedis, massages, hair treatments, beard grooming (if it applies)—the works. But don't stop there. Set the tone of a spa getaway by creating a fancy top-notch spa environment with all the amenities (such as robes, music, and refreshments) you'd expect from a five-star treatment.

What's the Word?

Making time to rest and recharge from your daily life is a necessary part of your connection to God. Being well-rested helps you do everything else you are called to do. Feeling rested in yourself and within your relationship makes you better people, able to handle the rest of your season as you move forward. Taking a day to indulge in spa treatments is one way to rest your mind and body. Giving God the heavy stuff that keeps you up at night is another. Be sure that as you take time off to rest physically, you also rest the worries of your mind and heart by indulging in some time with God.

Good For

- Honoring values
- Vulnerability
- Support

Tip

- Look up recipes for fancy foods and beverages, such as fruit-infused water, mini sandwiches, spritzers, and charcuterie boards.
- Set up a spa playlist so you can play relaxing music throughout your experience.
- Some people find it hard to indulge in self-care. Do what is comfortable for everyone. You and your date should create several spa options so neither of you has trouble selecting something that will relax and refresh you.
- Some spa sessions require supplies like oils, creams, and mud masks. If you can't invest in these products, research recipes to create them using items you already have, such as eggs, avocado, or extra-virgin olive oil.
- Massaging your date might be something you're into, especially when you're married, but if physical touch is too much for you or your date (or you're waiting to get physical), opt for different activities, like doing a hair conditioning treatment.

LEVEL UP

Schedule an at-home couples massage you both can enjoy simultaneously. Although most of these services are done within a spa-like facility, you may be able to get one in the comfort of your home. Book one for this date and relax together.

Talking Points

- How does your favorite spa station make you feel? How do you feel about this activity in general?

- Do you feel guilty pampering yourself like this? How do you feel about your date treating themselves?
- In a typical week, how often do you rest and relax?
- What keeps you from resting?
- Do any areas of your life make you feel weary or as though you are carrying a heavy burden?
- Are there any areas of the relationship that make you feel weary?
- How can you bring your burdens to God so you can rest?

GOD BLESS THE BIRDS

Look at the birds. They don't plant or harvest or store food in barns, for your heavenly Father feeds them. And aren't you far more valuable to Him than they are?

—Matthew 6:26

Build a birdhouse together to place outside your home. If you live separately, you can each decorate one so you can adorn both homes. You can build a birdhouse from scratch or buy a premade one and decorate it. If having birds in your yard isn't really your thing, consider decorating a birdhouse to display inside your home.

What's the Word?

If God takes care of all the birds, He shall surely care for you and all you encounter, including your relationship. In some cases, you may feel pressure to take matters into your own hands and try to solve the problems of your date, your relationship, or even yourself. Your worries are wasted time and energy. In Matthew 6:27, Jesus asks, "Can all your worries add a single moment to your life?" Rather than spending your moments in waste, give your worries to God to care for. If He can do so much for the birds, imagine all He and will do for you.

Good For

- Encouraging each other
- Teamwork
- Friendship

Tip

- Get creative with this project! Paint the outside of your birdhouse to really reflect your personality or your relationship. You can go wild with your imagination or paint it to match your own home.
- If you live in an apartment complex or have limited yard space, place your birdhouse (or even a bird feeder) near a window where you reside.
- Look up DIY bird feeders and houses you can create from scratch. For example, you can use a gallon-size milk jug to create a house, or add peanut butter and seeds to a pine cone to use as a feeder.
- Be mindful of other small animals (such as squirrels and chipmunks) that may try to get into your bird's living and feeding space.
- If birds aren't anywhere near your home, take this date outside. Feed some ducks or pigeons at a local park and bring some paper and colored pencils to make sketches of your feathered friends.

LEVEL UP

If you were a bird, what would you look like? With your date, paint a picture of a couple of "lovebirds," with you creating your version of one bird and your date creating the other. You can use these designs to personalize your birdhouse.

Talking Points

- How did it feel to take care of the birds?
- Do you feel like God is currently taking care of your needs?
- How can you take better care of each other?
- How can you both take better care of this relationship?
- Is there anything you worry about within your relationship that God is already taking care of?

THE POTTER AND THE CLAY

And yet, O Lord, You are the Father. We are the clay, and You are the potter. We are all formed by Your hand.

—Isaiah 64:8

Have some fun with clay! You can create your own work of art from scratch, like a bowl, mug, or vase, by shaping the clay with your hands and allowing it to dry. Or you can buy premade pottery that you and your date can paint. You can find starter kits at your local crafts store, along with a variety of YouTube videos to help you get started. You can each create your own item, such as a mug or a small bowl, or work on one together, like a vase or other larger piece.

What's the Word?

Clay comes in many forms. It becomes a sturdy work of art through baking, yet it can easily break into pieces and even shatter into dust. Think of yourself and your relationship as pottery—God is forming both into something good. Whenever something has been shattered within you or your relationship, God can revive it, carefully turning it back into something good, useful, and beautiful.

Good For

- Encouraging each other
- Trust
- Intimacy
- Vulnerability

Tip

- You will most certainly get your hands dirty, so avoid dangling sleeves and valuable jewelry, such as rings, watches, or bracelets.
- You can buy clay products online or at your local crafts store, along with paints, sculpting tools, and anything else you might need to tackle this date, whether you're a beginner or an expert. If it is your very first time working with clay, perhaps add an instructional book to your cart.
- Take your time with this date, allowing for two to four hours.
- Encourage your date. Tell them how great they are doing throughout this activity. Art is subjective, so there is no wrong way of doing it. Inspire each other, let your mind relax, and have fun!

- If you each make your own piece, use these items as gifts for each other so you are reminded of this date and the time and effort you and your partner put in.

LEVEL UP
Blindfold each other and mold a piece of clay using just your hands. Guiding your partner's hands will help shape an intimate work of art that's meaningful to both of you.

Talking Points

- What was the most challenging part of working with clay?
- How does working with clay remind you of God as He creates and shapes you?
- Did any part(s) of this date remind you of your relationship? How so?
- How can you work together to mold and create your ideal relationship?

THE BOB ROSS CHALLENGE

You must build this Tabernacle and its furnishings exactly according to the pattern I will show you.

—Exodus 25:9

The Joy of Painting, an early '80s TV show hosted by American artist Bob Ross, is enjoying a second life online. During his show, Ross created beautiful landscape paintings while giving a step-by-step tutorial with simple instructions. On this date, you will watch an episode together and reconstruct your own version of the painting using the careful, mellow teachings of Bob Ross.

What's the Word?

From the Garden of Eden to the heavens themselves to the Tabernacle where the spirit of God dwelled, everything God has made was created with exceptional detail. You, your life, and this relationship are no different. Every detail that makes you you, from how you like your eggs to how you show up in this relationship, is either designed and set in place for a reason or can be used in a unique way for God's perfect good. If you already understand this concept, you know the tiny details are what make this relationship and your connection so special. If you haven't discovered it yet, then it's time to dive into appreciating the details that make each of you a masterpiece.

Good For

- Encouraging each other
- Vulnerability
- Support
- Unconditional love

Tip

- Select an episode you think you'll both enjoy. You can find The Joy of Painting on YouTube, Hulu, and Amazon Video.
- You must obtain the right tools to create one of these paintings. As Bob Ross says in each episode, there's more to it than just paintbrushes! You also need an easel and the right paints. You can shop at a local crafts store or, better yet, purchase a Bob Ross painting kit online. You can also check out the blog post on getting the right tools for this date that is listed in the Resources section.

- This challenge requires patience and attention to detail. Take it slow and listen carefully. You can always pause and rewind the show if you need something repeated.
- Don't make it a competition to see who is the better painter. Rather, compliment your date on how well they are doing and let them know how much fun you are having with them.
- If possible, create a painting of a place you and your date would like to visit on a romantic getaway. As you paint, daydream about the trip together.

LEVEL UP

Unless you want to end up with two of the same painting, select two different episodes to watch (one on this date and another on a different date) so you each can paint a different picture, or paint the same painting using one episode and give away one to a friend or family member.

Talking Points

- How does this painting challenge make you feel?
- What details were most challenging to implement in your painting?
- What details within your relationship make it stand out and feel enjoyable?
- How can you apply the same patience, skill, and attention to detail from this challenge to your relationship?

CHAPTER THREE

Creative & Culinary

When you think of a date, it's often something like dinner and a movie. Sometimes changing the routine reveals a totally new side of you. That's why this chapter is filled with dates that are pleasing to the eye—and the stomach.

One thing to keep in mind whenever you are expressing yourself creatively or through food is that you have permission for that expression. Feeling insecure about what you create or what you eat (or don't eat) can lead to a tense and awkward date. What's important in these dates is that you affirm, reassure, and comfort your partner as they step into a place of inner expression and vulnerability. What they create can show you how beautiful they truly are on the inside in addition to their outer beauty. Likewise, the foods you and your date like, dislike, crave, or are willing to try for the first time can say a lot about your personalities.

Dates involving movies, crafts, music, and art will stir your heart with creative juices, and outings involving foods, treats, and cuisines are sure to awaken your taste buds. Together, these date ideas will tap into your senses of fun, delight, and pleasure. So look beyond the typical dinner date and see how much God will reveal to you regarding yourself, your date, and your relationship.

FARMERS' MARKET

Again, the Kingdom of Heaven is like a merchant on the lookout for choice pearls. When he discovered a pearl of great value, he sold everything he owned and bought it!

—Matthew 13:45–46

Visit a local farmers' market. Explore the vendors and observe what they are selling. Typically, you will find a plethora of produce, but you may also discover baked goods, sauces, coffee, and even nonfood items such as soaps, flowers, candles, bags, mugs, or home decor. Once you have thoroughly catalogued all that is offered at the market, select one food item and one nonfood item for the remainder of the date.

What's the Word?

Markets are filled with many options. At what point do you spot the value in something? Is a piece of fruit worth selling everything you have just to get it? How about a pearl? How about a spouse? When He made you, God knew you were special and rare. Can you say the same about your date and this relationship? Why is what you have in this relationship so special? If you can identify it, you will have an easier time keeping the relationship and treasuring it as something priceless.

Good For

- Respect and boundaries
- Honoring values
- Teamwork
- Honesty

Tip

- There is so much to explore at a farmers' market, so be sure not to rush. Browse each vendor at least twice and savor every moment.
- The food item you select could be an ingredient for a meal you can share later that day, or it could be a simple snack you both enjoy in the moment.

- For the nonfood item, get creative. You can find a lot of things at local markets. Just be sure whatever you select is something you can both enjoy.
- Observe what it's like to shop with your date. Notice how they choose the items they've selected. Are they a spender or a saver? Paying attention to their exploration will help you in other areas of the relationship.
- Aim to shop as local as possible. If there aren't any farmers' markets nearby, keep an eye out for garage sales or flea markets.

LEVEL UP

Get a reusable cloth bag you can decorate using paints, markers, or iron-on decals. Use your one-of-a-kind bag to collect your farmers' market items.

Talking Points

- How would you describe your experience at the farmers' market? Which items were most valuable to you?
- Of all the people who were "on the market"—that is, available to date—what made you decide to date each other?
- When it comes to shopping, what qualities do you typically look for in the items you buy?
- What qualities do you have to offer your date and this relationship?
- In a lifelong relationship, what values are you looking for?

KEEPING WITH THE TIMES

A time to cry and a time to laugh. A time to grieve and a time to dance.

—Ecclesiastes 3:4

Create a keepsake box that can hold your relationship's most precious moments. Once you find the perfect box for this date, decorate it together. Then collect everything that reminds you both of your flourishing relationship. You might include memorable items such as ticket stubs, photo booth pictures, menus, programs from theater performances, admission bracelets, pieces of clothing, dried flowers, and even a burned CD with songs from your early days together.

What's the Word?

Ecclesiastes 3:1 tells us, "For everything there is a season, a time for every activity under heaven." Some moments are good. Some are painful. God is still with us through it all—and so is His love. In your relationship, you'll have some great times and some really tough times. The key is to show up in your relationship and stand in faith, with love, no matter what. The keepsakes you've stored in your heart are very real reminders that God has brought you both through so much together, so you must continue to choose love even during difficult seasons.

Good For

- Valuing each other
- Honesty
- Unconditional love

Tip

- Use something sturdy for your box. You'll want it to last. A wooden box or a lockbox would be ideal, but ultimately you can choose anything you want.
- Add some written prayers to your box. They can be prayers you've said for each other and for your relationship. Bible verses that have encouraged you and uplifted you in your relationship are also great to include.
- If you are new to dating each other and don't have a lot to put into your box yet, start small. Each of you can place one item in the box that relates to your time together so far. Then include one prayer covering your relationship for the future seasons to follow.
- If you're married, make a copy of your wedding vows and place them into your box. If you can't find them, try to write them from memory (or come as close as you can). Use this time to recite your vows to each other.
- As you are placing memorable items in your box, use these moments to reflect together on what you've been through, what you enjoyed about those particular moments, and how each of them has brought you closer together.

LEVEL UP

Turn your keepsake box into a time capsule. Once you fill it with your relationship trinkets, place it in a waterproof bag and bury it. Set a date in the future when you will come together to open it again.

Talking Points

- Why are these particular items meaningful to you?

- What has been your most favorite relationship moment to date?
- What lessons have you learned along the way about each other?
- What lessons have you learned about yourself from the moments you've shared with your date throughout this relationship?

AN OLD FAMILY RECIPE

Direct your children onto the right path, and when they are older, they will not leave it.

—Proverbs 22:6

What does your family love to eat when they're gathered around the table? Is it Grandma's sugar cookies or Dad's summer barbecue ribs? On this date, you'll be taking on the challenge of replicating both the taste and the nostalgia of those family favorites as you re-create your family's most cherished recipes.

What's the Word?

What you share with your family can last for generations. Making and enjoying good food is a tradition that can not only bring your family together but also create lasting memories. Love shown through action is certainly something you can carry with you and pass on. More important than what you eat, or even how you show love, is sharing your faith in God. Whether you have been married for years or this relationship is just starting out, you are influencing someone through the way you love each other and God. If you talk with your loved ones about the loving God you know and how He has brought you and your partner into a loving relationship, they will cherish and share that story and faith with the generations to come.

Good For

- Honoring values
- communication
- compassion

Tip

- sometimes the cooking technique is just as important as the ingredients. Be sure to follow the recipe as closely as possible. This date isn't the time to add your own special touch to the dish. If you want to tweak it, do so the next time around. If possible, you may even want to ask the original chef or another family member for some trade secrets.
- Traditional recipes may bring a certain nostalgia into your date. Try to tap into each other's memories as the emotions arise.
- This dish could bring you closer to your date's family, and vice versa. If you're up for it, meet with some of your date's family members over this dish and enjoy it with them.
- Food and family run rich with culture. As you prepare this dish, get to know more about your date's culture, if different from your own, and how you can further embrace it. If the recipe belongs to your family, be sure to offer the same insights.

LEVEL UP

Both of you collect and combine all your family recipes and turn them into one recipe book that will be unique to your relationship, combining your shared traditions. Leave a few pages empty so you and your date can add some recipes of your own!

Talking Points

- What do you love most about the recipe you chose?
- What was it like in your house whenever this dish was made?
- How do you see you and your partner enjoying this recipe in the future?
- Along with this recipe, are there any other family traditions you want to bring into your relationship? What are they?

THE SMELL OF LOVE

The heartfelt counsel of a friend is as sweet as perfume and incense.

—Proverbs 27:9

Spend an evening with your date creating your own personal scent to wear on future dates. Get your date's input on what smells are most appealing to them, but ultimately you should select the fragrances that appeal to you most. See if there are any workshops in your area for making your own perfume. If you can't find one, there are plenty of online tutorials that show you how to use essential oils, flowers, and other aromatic ingredients to create the perfect scents. Don't forget to name your new favorite perfume!

What's the Word?

Smelling good is part of physical attraction, but stimulating one's mind is attractive, too! The Book of Proverbs tells us that smells and heartfelt counsel (compassionate advice and conversation) can equally satisfy and delight someone. In other words, it takes more than just looks and smells to delight the whole heart. Although you may like the way your date looks (and smells), the way you can really win them over time and time again is by showing up for them mentally, emotionally, and spiritually.

Good For

- Intimacy
- Romance
- Affection

Tip

- Bring some coffee beans on the date so you can cleanse your smell palate between sampling the various fragrances.
- The right perfume can increase your romantic feelings for your date, so get flirty and have some fun.
- Perfumes can mimic your natural pheromones, which can increase your body's chemical sex appeal. Wink, wink.
- Keeping this date within a group setting, like a perfume-making class, can help with setting physical boundaries if you are choosing to wait for physical intimacy.
- Turn your new scent into your official date perfume and wear it every time you enjoy a date!

LEVEL UP

Stretch your scent even further by mixing a few drops of your perfume into your oils and lotions. If you'd like to make your own soap from scratch, add a few drops of your perfume into any store-bought or homemade soap mix before allowing it to set.

use these items during intimate times, massages, baths, spa days, and the like.

Talking Points

- What fragrances did you enjoy most?
- What was the very first thing that attracted you to your date?
- What do you find most attractive about your date—not just physically, but mentally, emotionally, and spiritually as well?
- Recall a time when your date offered heartfelt counsel that left you feeling good.

FOREIGN FILM AND FOOD

For I was hungry, and you fed me. I was thirsty, and you gave me a drink. I was a stranger, and you invited me into your home.

—Matthew 25:35

Select a foreign film to watch together. You can do so at a theater or find a good movie to watch at home. Afterward, eat a meal related to the setting of your film. For example, if you watch a Japanese film, you might plan to eat sushi, ramen, or mochi ice cream afterward.

What's the Word?

It's not easy to feel like a stranger. Knowing what makes you feel out of place can help you know what to do to create comfort for yourself and others. God shows us that kindness and serving others with love, whether they are strangers or loved ones, is a great place to start. Next time you feel out of sync in your relationship, start developing a safe space by taking those first steps. Be kind to your date rather than assuming you know their intentions. Serve them with love without aiming to receive anything in return. You will be surprised at how these steps can defuse or prevent an uncomfortable situation.

Good For

- Respect and boundaries
- Vulnerability
- Honesty

Tip

- Start by selecting a film you would like to watch. There are thousands to choose from! First, determine which genre of movie you're in the mood for (romance, comedy, drama). From there, search the titles in your favorite streaming service, using the keyword "foreign" and your preferred genre. Give yourself 10 minutes (set a timer) to sift through the titles and select one that appeals to both of you. Once the timer sounds, you must come to a decision.
- Attending a local film festival may also give you a great variety of foreign films to watch. See if one is coming up in your area.
- Try to step out of your comfort zone with this date, both in learning about another culture and embracing that culture's cuisine. If you already love Mexican food, for example, go for something totally different.
- Foreign films aren't like typical American movies. Consider differences in story line, the length of the film, and how much explicit content there could be. Subtitles, too!

- Although the date itself may make you feel a bit out of your element, aim to keep your date comforted through conversation, laughing, and joking, and drawing toward each other to seek that bit of connection you may both be longing for.

LEVEL UP

Use Google Translate to learn a few phrases in the language of the film you chose to watch, and serenade your date!

Talking Points

- What was the most uncomfortable part of this date?
- What was the most fascinating part?
- If you felt out of place, what gave you comfort?
- How can you and your date work together to create a more comforting culture within your relationship?

WE ARE THE LIGHT

You are the light of the world—like a city on a hilltop that cannot be hidden.

—Matthew 5:14

Make candles with your date. You can do this activity at home with a kit you buy online or at a local candlemaking workshop in your neighborhood, if it's available. There is no set limit, no particular size or shape. As long as you are able to successfully light your candle by the end of this date, you have succeeded!

What's the Word?

God tells you that you are the light of the world. You are called to uplift and encourage, and love others, just as God does for us. Consider how many singles and couples around you can be blessed by seeing you shining your light! Regardless of whether you realize it, people are looking up to you in this very season. Be the light that God has blessed you and your date to be. By dating with God at the center of your relationship, you can inspire many others to do the same.

Good For

- Intimacy
- Romance
- Affection

Tip

- As exciting as this activity may sound, candlemaking requires patience. Do not rush the process. Rather, use the slower pace as a time to connect with your date.
- Not everyone is a candlemaking master. Compliment your date on their skills, regardless of the end result. Give yourself a bit of grace if your candle isn't up to par.
- Be mindful that a little fragrance in your candle can go a long way! Don't overdo it—you don't want to create a candle that is so overbearing you'll never want to light it.
- Speaking of fragrances, you can pair this date with "The Smell of Love" and create a candle using the fragrance you created for your personal perfumes.

LEVEL UP

Use your candles for those very meaningful moments of your relationship. Use them on the date when you decide to say "I love you" for the first time. Use them as part of your proposal if you decide to get married. Use them as a part of your marriage. Light them on your anniversary. Just think, the candles you make from this date can ignite the two of you on a lifelong journey of love!

Talking Points

- What do you like to use candles for?
- When was the last time you lit a candle? What was the occasion?
- How do you fill your life with light?
- How are you being a light to those around you?
- How can this relationship be a light to other couples?

CULTURAL FEST TOUR

The human body has many parts, but the many parts make up one whole body. So it is with the body of Christ.

—1 Corinthians 12:12

Celebrate the many cultures in your area by attending a series of cultural festivals. Participate in activities, enjoy a variety of foods, and dance to new music. Every weekend for three to five weekends (or more!), try to attend a different festival and enjoy the season learning and engaging in these cultures together with your date.

What's the Word?

People from all walks of life, from all over the world, are right in your own backyard! God created each of them to work together as one body, His church. You and your partner are also members and should therefore love and respect each other, working together for the glory of God. Who you encounter and how you choose to love (and be loved) will most certainly create a ripple effect that has the potential to lead others to God's love. Make it part of your relationship culture moving forward.

Good For

- Respect and boundaries
- Honoring values
- Friendship

Tip

- Check local news and social media sites to see when each cultural festival is taking place. Note the selected festivals on your calendar so you don't forget!
- Although many of the festivals will represent a demographic culture (Italian fest, Greek fest, Puerto Rican fest), pay attention to social cultures as well, such as music, art, and even medieval festivals.
- Although most of these festivals are free to attend, you'll need some money if you intending to purchase souvenirs or eat some good ol' festival food.
- These fests can get pretty crowded. Crowded places create the perfect reason for you and your date to hold hands. Doing so can connect you two on a deeper level throughout your date.

- You're bound to meet all types of people at these festivals. Why not strike up a conversation with someone to learn more about the festival?

LEVEL UP

For each festival you attend with your date, take home a small souvenir, such as a sticker, pin, or button, and start a collection you can add to throughout your relationship.

Talking Points

- For every festival you attend, discuss the differences and similarities you have with that particular culture.
- Which cultural festival taught you the most?
- Did you enjoy spending the day in a crowded event?
- Which part of the festival (food, music, activities, people) did you enjoy most?

COMING TOGETHER ONE PATCH AT A TIME

And we know that God causes everything to work together for the good of those who love God and are called according to His purpose for them.

—Romans 8:28

On this date, you are going to take crafting up a notch and test out your sewing skills. This task will be easy for anyone, whether you're an experienced sewer or just starting out. Create a quilt together that you can use on future dates. Use patches of fabric you and your date choose together while visiting a crafts store, or create your own patches using fabrics from other personal and meaningful items, such as old shirts or worn-out blankets.

What's the Word?

When God does a new thing in life, He has the power to create it out of nothing. The same is true of your relationship. Like the patches in your quilt, God was able to bring the two of you together to form something new. By caring for each other, you and your date can allow your relationship to become a blessing with many positive qualities. May this relationship (and the quilt) cover you, comfort you, and remind you that good can come out of God's beautiful creation.

Good For

- Teamwork
- Honesty
- Communication

Tip

- You can learn how to make a quilt through YouTube, blogs, or books. You can also try to find a quilt-making club or ask a family member or friend to teach you.
- You'll also need a sewing machine. If you don't own one, see if you can borrow one or buy a used one. You can also research quilters in your area who can make a quilt from the fabrics you select.
- Although your quilt doesn't have to have the perfect pattern, the design should make sense to you and your date. Work together to create a design that fits you and your relationship.

- Use your quilt during outdoor events, as a blanket to sit on during your picnics, or to cuddle under during a cozy night in. However you use it, the quilt should become a resource that will bring you two closer together.
- Make sure you create a quilt that is big enough to cover you both!

LEVEL UP

Create a quilt where the design and pattern of the quilt tells the story of your love and relationship. Use colors, patterns, and various shapes to describe how you met, and the most pivotal moments of your shared love.

Talking Points

- What do the patches on your quilt represent?
- Did you select a particular design or pattern? What does it represent?
- Which parts of the relationship have you contributed to?
- What values or qualities of the relationship make it better?
- Are there any patterns within your relationship that you enjoy?
- Do any patterns in your relationship need work?

DICE-COURSE MEAL

So go ahead. Eat your food with joy, and drink your wine with a happy heart, for God approves of this!

—Ecclesiastes 9:7

Let a set of dice help you plan your next meal! Roll a standard die. Whatever number it lands on, that is the number of courses you will have on your next dinner date. The higher the number, the fancier your dinner must be. Likewise, the lower the number you roll, the more casual you'll need to make it.

What's the Word?

Although you are blessed with many things in life (including this relationship), God can and is willing to bless you with so much more. Sometimes people have a hard time enjoying the blessings that come. God wants you to enjoy what He has already given you. He approves of you eating with joy and drinking with a happy heart. The next time God blesses you, your date, or your relationship, know that blessings come from God and are meant to be enjoyed, not downplayed.

Good For

- Trust
- Intimacy
- Romance

Tip

- If you roll high and decide to eat out, be prepared to spend a pretty penny. If you choose to dine in, do your research and know what kind of food must be served during a four-, five-, or even six-course meal.
- Agree that whatever the dice rolls is what you're going to stick to. That's what makes this date so much fun!

- For many, having a six-course meal might be a totally new experience, so make the absolute most of it—dress up, wear the pearls and fancy watch, pull out the chairs and hold open the doors, and enjoy yourselves!
- In case you were wondering what a one-course meal looks like, any one-pot or one-pan meal (see Pinterest or a recipe website) will do. Of course, enjoying a big plate of nachos works, too!

LEVEL UP

For the high-number rolls, try to recruit help, such as family and friends, to kick things up a notch. Have a friend serve as your chauffeur, or if you know someone who plays an instrument, have them play a song for you and your date to dance to.

Talking Points

- How did the unpredictability of this date make you feel?
- Which number did you secretly want to roll? Why?
- When you hear the phrase "the finer things in life," what comes to mind?
- How comfortable are you with the idea of living "fancy"? Explain your answer.

THE $20 DATE

If you are faithful in little things, you will be faithful in large ones. But if you are dishonest in little things, you won't be honest with greater responsibilities.

—Luke 16:10

Go on a date knowing that whatever you decide to do, you can only spend a total of $20 between both of you. Get creative and thrifty. Remember, a little can go a long way. The key is not to allow money to dictate the status or the enjoyment of your dates and your relationship.

What's the Word?

When you can be faithful with small portions, God will bless you with so much more in time. Consider the humble beginnings you and your partner had when you first began to date. By remaining faithful to each other and remaining faithful to God as a couple, you will reap God's rewards. First things first—cherish what you have in this season. Appreciate what God has already given you and your date within this relationship. In due time, you will both receive the upgrade of your heart's desire.

Good For

- Commitment
- Vulnerability
- Honesty

Tip

- Think outside of the dinner-and-a-movie box. The first step is to create a list of all the things you can do for free.
- Ice cream, $5 pizzas, coffee, fresh fruit, street nuts, and items from other vendors are all appropriate (and very inexpensive!) things you can enjoy on this particular date.

- Once you map out what you plan to do on your date, go out and enjoy it. Seriously! Don't let money (or lack thereof) get in the way of a great time. Go the extra mile with your commitment and bring only $20 in cash so you're not tempted to overspend.
- Keep your list of cheap dates after you've gone on this one. You never know when you'll want to do something spontaneous and inexpensive with your partner, especially if your funds are allocated elsewhere.
- You don't have to spend your money solely on food. Kites, bubbles, carnival games, admission to local and amateur shows, balloons, and flowers are all inexpensive items that can really jazz up your date in creative ways. What will you come up with?

LEVEL UP

Include a gift for your date within the $20 budget. Keep in mind that a gift doesn't have to cost a lot of money. A love letter, a flower, or another small trinket can really go a long way.

Talking Points

- If you can have this date with just $20, what would you do for a date that has a budget of $1,000? How about $10,000?
- Consider how you met. In what ways has your relationship gotten "richer" over time?
- Where would you like to see your relationship in the next year?
- Where would you like to see your relationship in the next five years?

CHAPTER FOUR
Outdoors & Adventure

When it comes to the great outdoors, every date can feel like an adventure. Even indoor public spaces like museums or shops can set the tone for just how adventurous your date can be. These settings give you the entire world as your playground to explore. They will reveal some things about you (and your partner) that you may not be able to discover while enjoying a cozy, comfortable night in. Contributing factors such as the weather, or other people, are completely out of your control.

These adventure-themed dates are here to remind you that control over your life is in God's hands, rather than yours. Ultimately, no matter how much you plan, external factors can affect the outcome in unpredictable ways.

When you're exploring somewhere new or stepping out of your comfort zone, rather than feeling anxious about things that may not go well, focus on the fact that you and your date are going to do something that will ultimately cause you to trust God even more. On dates, and in life, if your plans go off track, simply take it as God's way of encouraging you to lean on His plans instead. As a result, you and your date will grow and learn to trust each other more.

SERMON ON THE MOUNT

One day as He saw the crowds gathering, Jesus went up on the mountainside and sat down. His disciples gathered around Him, and He began to teach them.

—Matthew 5:1–2

Find a hill in your neighborhood where you and your date can go. If you can, climb to the very top. Once you get settled, set up a cozy space adorned with a nice blanket and perhaps a few refreshments. Then watch a sermon with your date on your phone or tablet. This date doesn't have to take place on a Sunday, and you don't have to watch a live sermon. Simply select a day that works for both of you and tune in to a sermon from your selected church.

What's the Word?

The Sermon on the Mount was perhaps one of Jesus's most talked-about sermons ever. Thousands of people came from everywhere to learn the values and faith-based lessons He was teaching that day. How awesome would it have been for you and your date to experience that moment? Although you cannot go back in time, you can share the teachable moment of learning those faith-based lessons and applying the valuable wisdom to your own life and your relationship.

Good For

- Honoring values
- Intimacy
- Being present

Tip

- Bring a blanket you don't mind laying on the grass or getting dirty.
- Make sure your smartphone or tablet is charged and that you have a good Wi-Fi connection or enough data to enjoy an entire sermon.
- Take notes (mentally or on paper) on what you've learned or gained from the sermon to discuss with your date afterward.

- Not sure how to find a hill? If there aren't any close by—say, at a local park—find a high-rise area (such as the top level of an apartment complex) where you can enjoy this date.
- Incorporate some of your favorite worship songs and prayers for each other into your date to make it a complete church service. Pray about the week ahead and how the sermon will speak to you.

LEVEL UP

You can read about the actual Sermon on the Mount (found in Matthew 5) and discuss the lessons Jesus preached about that day as you walk to your destination. What parts of Jesus's original Sermon on the Mount speak most to you?

Talking Points

- How did placing yourself in this environment remind you of Jesus and His Sermon on the Mount?
- Why did you decide to listen to the sermon you chose? Whose idea was it?
- What parts of the sermon you chose spoke to you most?
- Which speakers or pastors do you love listening to most? Why?

SHHH! THIS IS A LIBRARY!

Let all that I am wait quietly before God, for my hope is in Him.
—Psalm 62:5

Take a trip to your local library. Once you're there, each of you should select a book, a magazine, or another library item your date would enjoy. Once you've chosen something for the other to read, watch, or listen to, borrow those items from the library and exchange them outside. One last thing: this date will be held in a library, so you cannot speak during the entire duration of your date, but you can find other ways to communicate.

What's the Word?

Silence is a practice that can detach you from the noises of everyday life. It allows you to still your mind long enough to listen to deep thoughts. It can also allow you to focus more on what is being said without the use of words, through facial expressions and other forms of body language. When it comes to God, how much of what He is saying can be discovered and heard when you choose to remain silent? Likewise, what you choose not to say can also tell you a lot about the condition of your relationship. Let all your communication follow these two guidelines: choose to speak when necessary, and choose to listen always.

Good For

- Learning each other's interests
- Communication
- Being present

Tip

- Get a list of your date's favorite books to give you an idea of what they would like to read or listen to. But the final choice is yours!
- Make sure your library card is up to date and free from any library holds or late fees.

- Aim to speak as little as possible to your date. Instead, communicate creatively with your expressions and gestures.
- Feel free to browse around and get lost in the library. Be okay with exploring the shelves on your own or browsing together.
- If you're not sure what to choose, head over to the display table or bestsellers wall. There you will find new acquisitions, seasonal favorites, or the top New York Times bestsellers, all of which could yield some good recommendations.
- Libraries have more than books, too. If you're not big readers, you might be able to find an interesting audiobook, DVD, or CD for each other. Some libraries even have video games!

LEVEL UP

Now that you've found a perfect book for your date to enjoy on their own time, why not find a book you can read together? Before you leave the library, take some time (in silence) to find the perfect book for you and your date to enjoy as a couple.

Talking Points

- What's your favorite book of all time?
- Why did you select this book for your date to enjoy?
- What was it like not to speak during your date?
- What thoughts came to mind during your silent date?
- How often do you choose to be silent during your time with God?

OPEN HOUSE TOUR

A house is built by wisdom and becomes strong through good sense. Through knowledge its rooms are filled with all sorts of precious riches and valuables.

—Proverbs 24:3–4

Visit a few homes for sale that are hosting an open house so you and your date can take a tour of homes in your area (and perhaps a few that aren't local). During the tour, share with your date your likes, dislikes, and vision of what your dream house would look and feel like. Enjoy the adventure of imagining your future, either individually or together.

What's the Word?

Home is where the heart is. As your relationship continues, it will become a dwelling place for your dreams to mature and grow. Much like a house, you are building with your faith and your relationship a foundation that has a solid structure. In order to succeed, you must attain wisdom and good sense. From those key tools, your home, your relationship, and the place your heart dwells will be filled with loving valuables, sure to weather any storm.

Good For

- Encouraging each other
- Honoring values
- Vulnerability
- Unconditional love

Tip

- Use an app like Realtor.com or Zillow to find houses that are hosting an open house.

- You aren't really buying a home, so don't feel limited. Feel free to explore different houses of all budgets, sizes, and locations within your city!
- This date may spark some big-picture conversations. Be open to dreaming and sharing those dreams with your date.
- You can learn a lot about what your date values in a home. Pay close attention to their opinions and what excites them. Do not shy away from sharing your own perspective as well.
- Browsing houses for sale may give the impression that your relationship is headed in that direction. Before going on this date, make sure you are both on the same page in terms of where you stand and what this date is about so no one jumps to any conclusions.

LEVEL UP

Most people want to someday have a "forever home," and for many people that dream includes a "forever relationship." Make a list of all the things you and your date would like to have in your dream home and relationship. If you are already living in that forever space, create a list of what your home and relationship need to make them better. Together, pray over that list.

Talking Points

- What did you love most about the houses you saw together?
- What does your dream house have to have? Why?
- Is there anything you and your date can add or remove from your relationship in order to strengthen its foundation?
- How are you and your date using wisdom and good sense to build up your relationship?

THERE'S HISTORY HERE

Such things were written in the Scriptures long ago to teach us. And the Scriptures give us hope and encouragement as we wait patiently for God's promises to be fulfilled.

—Romans 15:4

Did you know there are more museums in the United States than McDonald's and Starbucks combined? Celebrate history by visiting a local museum together. It could be a natural history museum or a historical exhibit that focuses on your city or town. Have fun exploring, and as you are learning about the past, discuss with your date their history when it comes to love, relationships, and their faith.

What's the Word?

Not everyone is comfortable sharing their past, especially when it comes to relationships, breakups, and pain. By doing so, however, you can learn a lot about a person's history and how it has made an impact on them and their relationships. You each may have brought some past issues into your current relationship in the form of baggage (such as insecurity, mistrust, unbreakable walls). In order to heal, recover, and get past the past, you and your date must be willing to let go of the past and look forward to what lies ahead. Although you can't change the past and you have no real control over your future, the best thing you can do is trust God in the present. When you do so, your relationship will be exactly where it needs to be as God intended it so. Trust in this moment and this season.

Good For

....

- Trust
- Honesty
- Vulnerability
- Communication

Tip

- Prior to your date, check online for any museum information you may need to be aware of, such as ticket prices, parking, and hours.
- Most museums have seasonal exhibits that are special and unique. Research what exhibits might be coming so you can plan accordingly. You don't want to miss out on a one-of-a-kind experience.
- Bringing up the past may be difficult. Give your date some space if they choose not to go into full detail with some of their memories.
- Learning about history often brings awareness. Be open to the new things you many learn on your date and how your new discoveries may affect your relationship.
- You can't correct the past, but your actions and choices moving forward can make a huge impact. Set some relationship goals based on some of the new information you and your date discover about each other.

LEVEL UP

Each of you make a list of all the things from your past that you wish to leave in the past. At the end of the date, share your lists with each other, then destroy them by tearing them up or safely burning them.

Talking Points

- What were your past relationships like?
- What parts of your past involved pivotal moments in your life?
- Are there any parts of your future that worry you?
- How are you choosing to stay focused on the present?

X MARKS THE SPOT

Wherever your treasure is, there the desires of your heart will also be.

—Luke 12:34

Go on a treasure hunt with your date. You can both look for a surprise treasure together, using fun apps like Geocaching (an app that reveals real-world outdoor treasure hunts using GPS-enabled devices). Or you could create a treasure hunt for your date complete with clues, a treasure map, and, of course, a treasure waiting at the end.

What's the Word?

Finding treasure is exciting because we tend to look at treasure as something rare, valuable, and special. Such are the things you keep close to your heart. What you truly value in life—heirlooms, tokens of achievement, a job, even someone you love—is treasured within your heart and can be considered in favor above all else. Be sure that whatever you keep treasured is worthy of dwelling within your heart. Material things can fade away. Some relationships come and go, while others last forever. What you hold most dear should stand the test of time. Our treasures reflect our values.

Focus less on items that will fade away and more on the meaningful relationships that edify you in ways no solid treasure ever can or will.

Good For

- Honoring values
- Trust
- Communication

Tip

- Note that apps like Geocaching are often paid, and there is an unwritten rule of "take a treasure, leave a treasure." If you plan to use these apps to hunt for treasure, be prepared to leave a treasure as well. A simple toy, coin, keychain, or even a small note are acceptable options.
- If you plan to create your own hunt, start with the end in mind, then work backward to create the steps and clues.
- Whatever you decide the "treasure" should be, make sure it is something meaningful to your date and your relationship.
- Although we often think of treasure as something buried, this treasure doesn't have to be! If your date isn't open to the concept of digging a hole, find another unique place to hide your treasure.
- Mapping out a guided hunt will involve some serious planning. Give yourself a solid week to prepare all the steps, clues, and layout, and to create a map leading to the treasure.

LEVEL UP

Make every step or clue in the treasure hunt related to a memorable moment in your relationship. For example, if your first date was at an ice cream shop, write a clue that would lead your partner to the freezer, where they will find the ice cream flavor from that first date as well as the next clue.

Talking Points

- What was it like to hunt for treasure on this date?
- If you searched for treasure together, how did you work together?
- If you designed a treasure hunt for your partner, did you make it easy or difficult? What would your partner say?
- What emotions did you feel when you found the "treasure"?
- What are some things you treasure most in the world?
- Which relationships in your life have you treasured? Why?

FISHERMEN

Again, the Kingdom of Heaven is like a fishing net that was thrown into the water and caught fish of every kind.

—Matthew 13:47

It's time to go fishing! Grab your gear, get some bait, and visit a park, a lake, or another spot where fishing is allowed. Spend an afternoon (or morning) fishing together. Fishing equipment can sometimes be rented, and if you're totally new to this concept, hire a fishing guide who can navigate the way and teach you and your date the ropes. There are also loads of YouTube videos, instructional books, and other resources to help get you started.

What's the Word?

"There are plenty of fish in the sea." In the dating world, this phrase lets you know there are many people out there who could potentially be looking for what you're looking for. At some point, you are bound to catch feelings for one of those fish. And although ultimately we may seek to love just one fish, God has chosen to accept and love us all. No matter how unique we may all be in this great sea, God has every intention to love us all the same.

Good For

- Being present
- Communication
- Patience

Tip

- Find a local mom-and-pop bait shop to get your bait. You can also ask about the best places to go fishing in your area.
- Don't forget to check into fishing license regulations. Most states offer licenses online or at bait shops and sporting goods stores.
- Make the date silly by wearing funny hats, sunglasses, and rain boots during the entire fishing trip.
- The bait you use will largely determine the number and type of fish you catch. You can opt to go the traditional route or find the craziest bait possible (such as cheese or pickles) to see what the fish will like best.

- You might be out there a while waiting for the fish to bite, so play some card games or make a playlist you can listen to quietly during your fishing trip. (Or you can go through the Talking Points below!)
- If you and/or your date are absolutely not interested in catching real fish, get a board game that requires you to "fish," or grab some toys you can fish out of a tub or pool.

LEVEL UP

While at the bait shop, you and your date select a bait that reminds you of each other. Use these baits as a symbol for finally finding "a perfect catch."

Talking Points

- What did you enjoy most about this date?
- During the wait, what kept you calm until you finally caught a fish?
- What was it like to "wait" to find the "right fish" in your love life?
- How can you relate this fishing experience to how God gathers fish of every kind?

IT'S THE CLIMB

For He will conceal me there when troubles come; He will hide me in His sanctuary. He will place me out of reach on a high rock.

—Psalm 27:5

Today is all about the climb! On this date, you and your date must climb something. It could be a climb outdoors or a climbing wall at a recreation facility. Climb a hill, a tree, or even an actual mountain (if you live near one). Once you reach the top of your destination, enjoy the rest of your date with conversation and a special treat to celebrate.

What's the Word?

Mountains are tough to climb. Many times, your problems can feel like mountains and can stand in the way of progress in your life. Simply looking at the magnitude of the mountain you face can make you feel intimidated by its size and structure and stop you from climbing upward in order to reach the top. It can stunt your growth and keep you from reaching a place of peace and blessings. As you and your date climb your "mountains" today, always remember there is a way to overcome your problems. God will comfort you and place you on top of those mountains, away from the troubles and into a safe space where you can experience peace and success. But first you must be willing to climb.

Good For

- Trust
- Support
- Teamwork
- Commitment
- Communication

Tip

- This date will involve a lot of physical exertion, so wear comfortable clothing.
- The date can range from an indoor gym setting to an outdoor hiking setting, so the height of your climb can vary. Choose the

setting and challenge that will suit both you and your date.

- Be safe when climbing. Stretch, hydrate, and have a guide, if necessary, if you decide to tackle a challenging climb.
- As you pursue your climb, consider something that has been challenging your relationship or your role as a partner. Use this date and the climb as a metaphor for you to work together to overcome your struggles.

LEVEL UP

Climbing can often feel like you're actually leveling up. Pray together about how you and your date can reach the next level of your relationship. Are there any mountains in your relationship that are in the way? Before the climb, discuss these and think about them as you climb. Then revisit the conversation after you've reached the top. Have your perspectives changed?

Talking Points

- What was the hardest part of the climb? What did it teach you?
- How do you feel about taking risks now?
- How else can you show God you're ready to climb in life and in your relationship?

100-MILE DATE

Do not be afraid or discouraged, for the Lord will personally go ahead of you. He will be with you; He will neither fail you nor abandon you.

—Deuteronomy 31:8

Look at a map and take note of all the towns and interesting places within a 100-mile radius of your home. Maybe there's a location you've always wanted to see but you've never had the opportunity to go there. Maybe you'll discover a little out-of-the way place that seems interesting. Once you choose your route, pack up your car, fill your gas tank, and take a day to go on an adventurous road trip to visit some of the places you'd like to explore.

What's the Word?

Sometimes God will call you to go to places beyond what is comfortable. You have to explore new settings and regions. Much like a relationship filled with uncharted places, God will always be with you in your exploration. Even better, He goes before you to those places and will keep you safe, grounded, and within His will if you decide to trust and follow Him. But you cannot explore any of what God has prepared for you until you take the first step of trusting Him. Then you can take action in the direction He is leading you.

Good For

- Respect and boundaries
- Trust
- Unconditional love

Tip

- This date might take you into a new town or even a new state! Be prepared for the day trip with regard to mealtimes, phone chargers, gas stops, and snacks.

- You never know what you'll find 100 miles from your home. Be open to anything! You might come across shops, museums, restaurants and diners, parks, cities, lakes, even oceans. Anything is possible.
- Prior to the date, do some research on your destination so you have a loose plan to follow once you arrive. But don't be afraid to explore and get a little lost.
- This date doesn't actually have to be 100 miles away. If you're not big on road trips, it could look like a simple visit to the next town over with plenty of stops along the way. Whatever makes sense for you and your date to do, enjoy it and have fun.

LEVEL UP

Plan on making a photo album or scrapbook dedicated to this trip as a way to remember your shared adventure. You could include a map of the destination highlighted, rest stop receipts, souvenirs, shells from a beach, or anything else you found along the way that will spark your memory of the day.

Talking Points

- How did you choose your destination(s)?
- What about the trip surprised you? What disappointed you?
- What about this date was exciting or scary?
- Where do you think this relationship is headed next? What's exciting about it? What's scary?
- Did you feel that God was ahead of you on this journey? Where did you feel Him?

DEEP WATERS

> When you pass through the waters, I will be with you. When you go through rivers of difficulty, you will not drown.
>
> —Isaiah 43:2

Spend a delightful day venturing into deep waters with your date. Choose an activity that suits both of you, whether you're feeling adventurous (waterskiing, surfing) or you're in the mood to relax (canoeing or kayaking), just as long as you are not in shallow waters simply skipping rocks on the shore. Whatever you decide, make sure it's enjoyable and fun for both of you.

What's the Word?

God wants you to trust in Him. As you experience your time in the water, seeing how it moves and how you move in it, reflect on the measure of faith God is calling you to have in order to go deeper with Him. It may feel a bit scary to have no idea where that trust in God will lead you. Much like this date, going into deep waters can also feel risky—that is, if you don't have the proper supports, like a life vest or a boat that will not sink. The same can be said about your faith in God. He is the life preserver that cannot sink, no matter how deep you are willing to go or how far He is willing to take you. You may also need to have more faith in your partner and the two of you as a unit in order to go deeper in your relationship. God is there to keep your life and your relationship safe and steady, even in fast, turbulent waters.

Good For

- Trust
- Honoring values
- Commitment

Tip

- Plan to do something at a body of water near you. You may have multiple options, so decide on the activity first.
- Read the story of Peter walking on water (Matthew 14:22–33) and discuss what it would be like to physically walk on water toward Jesus. What is God showing us in this moment?
- As you physically venture into deeper waters, be open to having deeper conversations with your date to increase intimacy.
- You and your date should both select one deep topic (like finances, marriage, relocation, job changes, growing in faith) to discuss. As a jumping-off point, try thinking of one question about the topic and posing it to your date. By the end of the date, be sure you were each able to touch on the chosen topic.
- On this date, you will probably get wet. Be prepared with towels.

LEVEL UP

Write a prayer together that lifts up whatever deep waters you and your date are currently facing. In the prayer, ask God to increase your faith, build your trust, and help you discover ways that you and your partner can come together through these issues.

Talking Points

- Are you a water person? How comfortable are you in the water? Why or why not?
- What did it feel like to move through deep waters?

- How can you and your partner gain more mutual trust in order to move through the deeper levels of your relationship?
- How can you trust God more when it comes to the deeper parts of this relationship? of your faith?
- What can you do to trust each other more when it comes to growing deeper in your relationship?

RELATIONSHIP RETREAT

Then Jesus said, "Let's go off by ourselves to a quiet place and rest a while." He said this because there were so many people coming and going that Jesus and His apostles didn't even have time to eat.

—Mark 6:31

Create a one-day retreat where you and your date go away to a secluded place, such as a tent or a small cabin, and truly unplug from the stress of the modern world. Turn off your phones and start your retreat with a relationship devotional, and create activities that allow you to spend one-on-one time together alone and discuss your relationship in detail throughout the day. Plan to have meals and snacks on this retreat. Also, like many retreat settings, plan to have several fun activities (like making s'mores together) and play a couple of board games before heading into the heart of your relationship. End the retreat by praying and worshipping together.

What's the Word?

Sometimes the business of the days and seasons will cause you to move without rest. Rest is required for all people to think clearly, draw near to God, and seek to know His plans. Much like the rest that is required for our physical, emotional, mental, and spiritual needs, it is also necessary to create rest within your relationship. Giving your relationship a chance to get away from distractions, and to recharge (or recover) from any strains you both may have been struggling with, will become a key factor in working toward a sustaining, healthy, and satisfying relationship.

Good For

- Being present
- Communication
- Teamwork
- Honesty
- Commitment

Tip

- Plan for this date to take up the entire day. Dress appropriately for outdoor weather and get plenty of rest the night before.
- This retreat is meant for you to focus on your relationship. Bring up topics you would like to work on and commit to focusing on them throughout the day.
- Some retreats involve trust exercises, brainstorming sessions, and teamwork-building activities. Incorporate any of these activities.
- This date is a great way to help you grow intimately with your partner. Incorporating little ways to increase your emotional intimacy, such as exchanging compliments or hugging a certain number of times, can help you do so in a way that goes beyond the bedroom.

- Create a set of rules you must both follow throughout your retreat to maintain focus and respect, like no phones and no interrupting when the other person is speaking.

LEVEL UP

Bring along a couple's book you can read from and apply during your retreat.

Talking Points

- What was your biggest takeaway from this retreat?
- What are you most excited to implement in your relationship moving forward?
- Why does God encourage us to retreat and rest?

CHAPTER FIVE

Together in Service

Some of the most unique kinds of dates I recommend for Christian couples are those where you can serve together. Service dates are how my husband and I grew to love each other on a deeper level and display our love for God at the same time. My husband and I met in church, which was very traditional. But dating while also choosing to honor God in a secular world was a bit of a challenge. The loophole we found was spending time together through acts of community service.

What I love most about service dates is that they are so pure and full of good intentions. There are no secular motives when you are serving someone beyond yourself. Giving back to your community together takes you beyond the dating bubble. You learn less about what your date thinks about you and more about what they think of the world and those in it. Revealing those tender parts of the heart can be just the thing that shows you the person you are dating is truly special.

You may think a service-oriented activity would take away from you spending close time with your date. But I can assure you, the date will leave you both feeling closer. Know that you must be willing to consider others. As you are doing so, revealing your servant heart will lead your date to consider you more than ever before.

SPARE CHANGE

If you help the poor, you are lending to the Lord—and He will repay you!

—Proverbs 19:17

On this date, create small care packages that you and your date can give to the homeless. Start by collecting resourceful items, such as socks, gloves, hand sanitizer, granola bars, tissues, and gift cards. Then create care packages by placing your items in plastic bags and storing them in your car or bag for whenever you're on the go. Creating these kits together provides a nice opportunity for you and your date to share your values with each other. You can even make a date of it by taking a walk or a drive and looking for anyone asking for spare change, then handing them one of your care packets. Create as many of these packages as you like.

What's the Word?

God loves all people. He loves when His people help and are generous to others. When you are generous with others, you unveil a special piece of your heart—not just to your date or the person you are serving, but also to God. There is more to life than your relationship. Helping others can be a gentle reminder of this fact and can pull you into that generosity on a regular basis. The heartfelt gestures you and your date make together can define your relationship with a genuine love that goes beyond each other and spills over onto other people.

Good For

- Honoring values
- Compassion
- Being present

Tip

- Include items that will not perish, melt, or go bad. Think of shelf-stable items that are easy to carry, lightweight, and healthy.

- Make your packages no bigger than a gallon-size plastic bag. The goal is to create multiple packages so they are readily available to distribute to those in need.
- Always approach people with respect, humility, and love. This date is not about garnering social media likes, and you don't have to publicize it. It's about better loving and serving others together.
- Together with your date, write Bible verses and/or words of encouragement on index cards to include in your care packages.
- Handing out your care packages is meant to be a quick exchange, but do not shut down an opportunity to engage and talk with those whom you're serving if they extend the invite for conversation.

LEVEL UP

Together with your date, ask if anyone you're serving would be open to receiving prayer. Then pray over them as a couple.

Talking Points

- Why did you select the items to go in your care package?
- How did it feel to interact with the homeless and those in need?
- Can you see you and your date serving this population again? Why or why not?
- How has caring for the homeless brought you closer to your date?
- How has caring for the homeless brought you closer to God?

THEIR BIGGEST FAN

So encourage each other and build each other up, just as you are already doing.

—1 Thessalonians 5:11

On this date, you and your date will become cheerleaders for a charity event. Select a public event, such as a marathon, a 5K, or a charity basketball tournament, that supports a cause close to your heart. Make signs of encouragement prior to the event and hold them up while cheering for the participants as they set out to complete their acts of physical service for good cause.

What's the Word?

When facing a difficult task, nothing feels better than receiving encouragement from others. Even if you're not participating in the event directly, you're doing a great service by helping the participants reach the finish line. God loves us and supports us this way, too—He is our biggest cheerleader, and He calls us to encourage others as well. Sure, being a cheerleader for a sporting event is fun, but becoming a cheerleader for your partner, supporting them through their various trials and challenges, is truly serving God. When you encourage others, whether it be strangers or those you love, you build each other up and everyone wins.

Good For

- Encouraging each other
- Playfulness
- Teamwork

Tip

- If there is a specific race or charity event you are looking to cheer for, contact the organizer and get the details on when to show up and where to go. You may also need to preregister or get permission from the organization.
- Use upbeat music from your phone and a small Bluetooth speaker to kick up your excitement a notch. Dance, jump, pump your fists, and bring the heat!
- Paint each other's faces to show off your team spirit.
- If allowed, hand out cups of water to the participants as they pass you by. (But remember to ask the event organizer first.)
- Arrive early enough to set up your post before the first participant arrives. Likewise, do not leave your post until the very last one passes by. Keep up your high energy and encouragement from beginning to end.

LEVEL UP

Make matching T-shirts for you and your date to wear during the event. You can tie-dye them, use iron-on stickers, or jazz them up with fabric markers.

Talking Points

- How did it feel to encourage strangers passing you by?
- Do you feel like cheering for others also helped the cause itself? Why or why not?
- When was the last time you said something to encourage your date?

- What was the last thing you remember your date doing or saying to help build you up? How did it make you feel?

ANIMAL AFTERNOON

The godly care for their animals, but the wicked are always cruel.
—Proverbs 12:10

With your date, visit your local animal shelter and volunteer to spend time with the animals. It may not mean cleaning out cages and dealing with the messy work. Ask if you can play with animals, take them on walks, or simply cuddle them outside of their living spaces. Spend an entire afternoon at the shelter.

What's the Word?

Not only does God care for people, but He also cares for animals. Now it's your turn. Adopting an animal may be a big commitment for both of you, but going together to care for those who need it can do more than just ease an animal's burden. It also offers you and your partner an opportunity to do God's will by pouring some of the love you share into another one of God's beautiful creations.

Good For

- Compassion
- Honoring values
- Playfulness

Tip

- Some animal shelters offer this type of volunteer service already. Call in advance to see if you can participate or drop in one afternoon.
- This date is a great way to explore how you both feel about pets. For couples who have been together a long time, it may reveal changing attitudes about pets, too. It is a great opportunity to get on the same page about a big issue.
- Wear comfortable shoes in case you go for a dog walk. Also, be sure to wear clothing that you wouldn't mind getting a bit dirty or covered in pet hair.
- Pay attention to how your date nurtures the animals they are spending time with. They might reveal a softer side of themselves you haven't seen before. Or maybe animals aren't for them, but they're trying their best. That's okay, too!

LEVEL UP

Before your visit, make some homemade treats together with your date that you can give to the animals you plan to love on. Do research beforehand or check with the shelter to make sure the animals can safely digest the ingredients.

Talking Points

- What is your favorite animal and why?
- How did you feel about caring for the animals? What was the most challenging part?
- Are you open to caring for animals more consistently in the future, either by visiting and volunteering more often, or by sponsoring/adopting an animal of your own?
- What can you and your date decide to do to care for God's animals on a continual basis?

FUN IN A BOX

Pure and genuine religion in the sight of God the Father means caring for orphans and widows in their distress and refusing to let the world corrupt you.

—James 1:27

Create a "box of fun" that you can donate to a local group home. You can fill your box with toys and games. The size of the box is up to you. The date will consist of you selecting the toys that will go inside the box, then delivering it to your location. You can also include a note with some edifying words for the children.

What's the Word?

Several times in the Bible it is mentioned that God loves and cares for the orphan child. He desires for you to care for them, too. Regardless of whether you're looking toward marriage and possible future children, you can still use this particular date to care for and show love to others. When you provide new ways for children to engage in a bit of fun, you are helping create a moment where kids can just be kids. And if you and your date can use your time together to help serve others, your goals will always be in alignment with God's will.

Good For

- Honoring values
- Compassion
- Playfulness

Tip

- You can create themed boxes (like art, music, or sports), or simply pick whatever you want to put in a random box of fun!
- Decorate the outside of your box using paint or wrapping paper to spruce it up and increase the fun.
- Keep candy and/or food out of your box because you don't know what the kids can or cannot have.
- Call ahead before you drop off your box to learn about the rules of the group home before you head that way.
- The more, the merrier! Ask other friends to create their own "fun in a box" that you can pick up with your date and deliver to the group home.

LEVEL UP

Is there a way for you and your date to volunteer within the group home? Can you serve as a mentor for the day? Look into ways to get involved on a deeper level.

Talking Points

- Why did you pick these particular toys and games for the box?
- Are you open to foster care or adoption in the future?
- If fun came in a box for you, what would that fun look like?
- What other ways can you care for children in need, as God has instructed?

COMMUNITY WITHIN REACH

> Don't be selfish; don't try to impress others. Be humble, thinking of others as better than yourselves. Don't look out only for your own interests, but take an interest in others, too.
>
> —Philippians 2:3–4

churches often have a team that conducts regular outreach programs throughout the year. They may even have an entire schedule of events for serving the community. one outing could be cleaning up a yard of a community member. Another event could be cooking and distributing a meal. or the church might simply decide to serve with random acts of kindness, handing out free water bottles and granola bars to those passing by. with a church of your choice, sign up together to volunteer in the next community outreach event.

What's the Word?

when you go to church, you are most likely going to help yourself grow and connect spiritually. when you leave the church afterward, you should be inspired to help others grow and connect. By joining an existing team whose members are also inspired to serve, love, and grow, your two-person team will inevitably follow suit as you progress in your relationship. why not use your connection with each other to advocate for the interests of others and help strengthen your community?

Good For

- Honoring values
- Teamwork
- support

Tip

- You may need to attend some outreach meetings leading up to the event. Be sure to connect with the community outreach director or ministry leader so you are aware of what you need to do in order to attend and participate in the event.
- You will probably be given a role to fulfill during the event. You may even have to do something completely different than your date. Come with a humble heart and serve where you can.
- There might be various ways to help your church serve in the community. Discuss with your date which event speaks most to you and volunteer for it together.
- Serving your community might be tougher than you think. Be okay with talking to strangers, praying in groups, and working hard with others for the good of the cause.
- People within your group may ask about your date and your relationship. Make sure you and your date are comfortable sharing that information if you are questioned.

LEVEL UP

Although community outreach events are usually a group thing, you can always meet with your date before or after the event for some one-on-one time to chat, grab coffee, or prep for your outreach date.

Talking Points

- What did you like most about this outreach date?
- Were there any challenges in working with others to serve the community?
- Which part of this date pulled you out of your comfort zone?
- Why do you believe God wants you to look out for others?

- How did it feel to be seen by others of your church as a couple?

THE BABYSITTER'S CLUB

Children are a gift from the Lord; they are a reward from Him.

—Psalm 127:3

There's no doubt about it: children are gifts from God. But sometimes parents need a break, and they aren't always blessed to have a sitter available. On this date, you and your date will volunteer to babysit for friends or family members so they can enjoy a well-deserved date night of their own.

What's the Word?

Whether you and your date have children of your own or are thinking of having them someday, there are always ways to express your love for children. Allowing your friends or family members a chance to work on their own relationships, without kids, is one way you as a couple can bless them. But do not overlook the fact that all children are gifts from God as well. In other words, although you are blessing the couple with this act of service, the time you and your date spend engaging with their children will also serve as a blessing to you. This date may gift you and your partner in ways you never expected.

Good For

- Respect and boundaries
- Honoring values
- Teamwork
- Communication

Tip

- If you do have kids, turn this babysitter date into a playdate if the parents are agreeable to it.
- If they don't know both of you well, the parents might feel uncomfortable having both you and your date at their house during an evening out. If so, propose that they have a day date or a date that would best suit their comfort level.
- Kids require lots of time and attention, so be ready to focus on them. Aim to spend minimal time on your phone and in front of the TV (unless that is all the kids want to do!).
- How you resolve conflict among the kids may be different than how your date would handle things. Make sure you work together and demonstrate healthy, loving conflict resolutions in front of the kids in your care.
- It's okay to flirt, but keep your behavior G-rated.

LEVEL UP

Bring a bag filled with snacks, games, and other goodies that you, your date, and the kids can enjoy together.

Talking Points

- Why do you believe children are so important to God?
- What was the best part of this date? What was challenging?
- Do you see yourself having kids in the future? Did your opinion about having kids change at some point? Why?
- What was one thing, as a sitter, you wanted to make sure happened during your time caring for the kids?

- What qualities or traits do you look for in a parent of your current or future children?

EVERGREEN ELDERS

Never speak harshly to an older man, but appeal to him respectfully as you would your own father. Talk to younger men as you would to your own brothers. Treat other women as you would your mother, and treat younger women with all purity as you would your own sisters.

—1 Timothy 5:1–2

Choose an older friend or acquaintance from church to love and serve with your date. For this particular date, help your elder by taking care of their yard. You and your date can mow the lawn, pull weeds, fix their flower beds, shovel snow from their driveway, or rake leaves. If you and your date are approaching your elder years yourself, seek out another friend or acquaintance who could use some assistance with certain tasks.

What's the Word?

The elderly are to be treated like your parents, according to the Bible. We are called to honor our parents (see Exodus 20:12); therefore, we must honor the elderly. They cannot always do for themselves what they did in their prime, so you and your date must take it upon yourselves to care for them and help them create a space they can be proud of. When you and your date can pour out love over those who are older, you can catch a glimpse of what that love will look like in each other as you grow older together.

Good For

- Honoring values
- Teamwork
- compassion
- support

Tip

- The elder person you choose to serve does not have to be a relative or close friend. They could be a neighbor, someone from your community, or another individual you feel pressed to serve.
- come equipped with all the landscaping gear you will need for this date. The person you're serving may not have all the tools.
- You can learn a lot by observing how your date treats the elderly. Pay close attention, as their actions may show you how they will care for the elders in your life today (or for you, if you choose to spend your lives together).
- some elders crave company. If you and your date are okay with it, stick around to chat if they extend the invitation. You'll all benefit from the fellowship, and you may gain some great wisdom for your relationship by listening to what they have to say.
- spruce up their yard with a lovely birdhouse, some new colorful flowers, or a joyful lawn ornament!

LEVEL UP

Together with your date, bake some homemade cookies and write prayer-filled, friendly letters you can leave with your elder.

Talking Points

- What was it like gardening or landscaping with your date? How well were you able to work together to get the job done?
- What was it like to serve the elderly?
- Why would God instruct you to care for the elderly as you would care for your own parents?
- How do you normally care for the elderly in this current season?
- How would you want to be treated as an elder someday?
- Do you have any elder loved ones who are important in your life?

WE ARE THE CHURCH

Therefore, whenever we have the opportunity, we should do good to everyone—especially to those in the family of faith.

—Galatians 6:10

There are a lot of ways to be involved in a church. As mentioned earlier, many churches have a ministry that gives back through community outreach. But what about all the ways you can serve within the church, benefiting the people who come each week? On this date, you and your date should commit to serving on a ministry within the church for a season. It can be any ministry (such as children's services, youth group, hospitality, media, worship team or music ministry, drama team, prayer team, greeters) as long as you and your date can serve together.

What's the Word?

It takes a lot to serve in a church setting. Although this service-based date may be a blessing for others, it will also become a major blessing for you and your date over time. Joining any ministry within a church is a great way to do good for your family in faith. It will help with the upkeep of the church, and it will help you grow together in a setting that can become a second supportive group for your relationship. But that's not all. Serving on a ministry together will also fill you and your date spiritually on a regular basis. You will in turn grow to love each other inwardly while also inspiring those around you as you demonstrate your love and devotion toward each other and God.

Good For

- Honoring values
- commitment
- communication
- support

Tip

- There are many church ministries to choose from. For this particular date, start with one that is not too time-consuming, and consider committing to serving on it once a month.
- Serving on a ministry requires a semi-long-term commitment. Aim to serve on the same ministry with your date for at least three months.
- During your time together, remind yourself that although it's exciting to meet your date on these ministry dates, you are ultimately serving God by serving in His church. Focus on the ministry first and your date second.
- As you serve more, you'll come to notice things you like and dislike in certain ministries. Over time, encourage your partner to serve in the church ministry that best fits their gifts and passions.

- Learn how to get comfortable loving and serving each other in a church setting. It's okay to hold hands, laugh, and engage with each other as a couple in a relationship. As long as your intentions and affections are pure, it is okay to act like a couple.

LEVEL UP

Before your ministry date each month, get together before the church service and pray together that your time serving will be blessed, and that together you and your relationship will grow.

Talking Points

- Which church ministry makes you feel joyous?
- Which ministry do you feel isn't the best fit for you? Why?
- How do you feel dating within a church setting?
- Is there any part of this date that makes you uncomfortable? If so, what?
- In what ways do you desire to serve God in the future?

CHAPTER SIX

Group Dates

This chapter is all about doubling the fun with others. Although there is so much to explore during one-on-one time with just your date, you can discover even more when you include your family and friends. How you interact with them and how they perceive you can teach you both a lot about yourselves and your relationship. Engaging with these other relationships in your lives can reveal blind spots you never knew you had. The people closest to you can see parts of you (or your date) that you often can't see yourself. Including these folks on a date or two taps into a totally fresh and new perspective that can inspire you to establish an even better relationship with your date.

Could it get awkward to share a date with your parents or kids? Absolutely. But they might be able to see something in you or your date that could change everything. Should you include dates with the friends you grew up with? Of course! Knowing what it's like to share life with friends and the one you're dating can determine whether your most beloved relationships will complement each other. Do you think you're ready to dive with your date into the existing relationships that mean most to you? There's only one way to find out. Here are a few ideas to get you out of your relationship bubble and into a world where all your most favorite people can coexist in peace, love, and harmony!

NETFLIX AND GRILL

They worshipped together at the Temple each day, met in homes for the Lord's Supper, and shared their meals with great joy and generosity.

—Acts 2:46

On a warm day, gather your friends together along with your date for an outdoor meal. Spark up the grill and host a good old-fashioned barbecue, complete with all the grilled favorites. You and your date will create the menu, set up the yard, plan the activities, and invite several of your friends to come together for the occasion. After the festivities, set up your TV for a group viewing of a movie or your favorite show.

What's the Word?

Fellowship among friends can be a valuable part of your life. It creates a gladness in your hearts and produces healthier and stronger bonds over all levels of relationships. Yes, growing close to your date is important. Creating an environment where you can appreciate all the relationships you cherish together is truly a blessing. Knowing that God has brought you together in friendship and love is special—just imagine all God is going to do with this particular connection. Consider all the ways your circles of influence can help each other grow in faith and encourage one another to love like God. You must strive to build a life where loved ones and the one you love can meet, break bread, and share joy and generosity together.

Good For

★ Playfulness
★Friendship★
Support

Tip

- Make this barbecue a potluck-style meal so you and your date aren't responsible for preparing all the dishes. Reach out to your friends and ask them to bring a side dish, beverage, or dessert. You and your date can concentrate on the main courses.
- Invite between four and six friends so you can have meaningful conversations with everyone.
- Use your favorite streaming service or rent a movie. You can set up a viewing inside, or watch outdoors using a projector or hooking up your TV!
- It can be nerve-racking for your date to meet your friends because they know you so well. Remember to be yourself, stay clear-headed, and have fun. Don't stress too much about it being a "date"—the key is for everyone to get to know one another.
- Create a space where you and your date would feel comfortable bringing your friends together. Make sure that your arrangements cater to everyone.

LEVEL UP

Turn your evening group date into an overnight binge and allow your friends to stay all night long!

Talking Points

- Is there anything you learned about your date by getting to know their friends?
- How often do you enjoy hanging out in a group setting?
- Were there any challenges having your friends and your date's friends hang out in the same space?
- What does it mean to you to have godly friends?

- How can you turn the friendships you established on this date into godly friendships moving forward?

CHURCH HOP

For they are transplanted to the Lord's own house. They flourish in the courts of our God.

—Psalm 92:13

Is going to church every Sunday important to you or your date? Perhaps you met in church and have attended the same one throughout your relationship. Maybe you both go regularly but to different churches. Or maybe going to church is new for you both. This date is meant to allow you to honor the value of faith together as a couple. Each Sunday for a month, visit a different church together along with your friends or loved ones and share your experiences with each other afterward. You can choose from a variety of options. Maybe you visit the church you grew up in, check out one that a family member or friend attends, or try an intriguing new one you've been meaning to visit.

What's the Word?

Attending a church helps you engage with other Christians. It can help you grow your faith while fulfilling God's desire for you to love and serve others. Perhaps you have gone to one church your whole life and everyone there knows everything about you. Maybe you found a church while you were still single and searching to date someone new. These settings and environments may cater to you, but do they now cater to your date and relationship as a whole? Using the connection of friends and family could allow you to explore a church setting that you and your date will love and never would have discovered on your own. Finding a place that will allow you and your date to grow spiritually together will help your relationship truly flourish.

Good For

- Encouraging each other
- Honoring values
- Support

Tip

- Look online for churches you and your date may be interested in attending. Together, narrow the list down to four or five.
- Commit to attending each church you selected. Don't get comfortable with one church just yet. Be open to seeing what's out there, and take into account the various styles of worship, the preaching and sermon topics, and the church culture.
- You may discover that you and your date enjoy different church cultures. At the end of this multi-series date, continue to attend the church that brings you both the most fulfillment as a couple.
- If you don't usually attend a church service, check out the church's website prior to your visit so you know what to expect.
- Attending in person can reveal a lot more about the establishment than simply watching online. Likewise, a Friday service can have a totally different feel than a Sunday first service. Consider these factors when you are planning your visit.

LEVEL UP

After each service, enjoy some coffee with your date and share your thoughts about the service you just attended.

Talking Points

- What did you like about each church? What did you dislike?
- What do you look for in a church home? Why?
- How often do you attend church?
- What are some of your defining experiences with church?

MEET THE PETS

Then God said, "Let us make human beings in our image, to be like us. They will reign over the fish in the sea, the birds in the sky, the livestock, all the wild animals on the earth, and the small animals that scurry along the ground."

—Genesis 1:26

Some people are pet lovers. Are you? Is your date? Lots of people think of their pets as close family members, and it's important to respect such a relationship if it exists for your date. Spend a day loving on the pets in your life with your date. Use your time together to play with them, give them a bath, take them for a walk, and clean their bed and living space. If you are a couple who already share a household and a pet, spend this date loving on that pet in your life!

What's the Word?

God created man and woman last. Before the creation of people, He made animals of every kind. Adam and Eve's first job was to have dominion over the animals. Some of those animals have come to be our most cherished companions. Learning about this particular relationship, if it exists for you or your date, will help you know how to share your date in this setting. Much like how Adam and Eve learned to live in harmony with the animals in the Garden of Eden, this date will allow you to see how you can all come together as family.

Good For

★ Vulnerability
★Commitment★
Boundaries

Tip

- ★ If you and your date both have dogs, consider an outdoor activity like going to a dog park or enjoying a long walk.
- ★ If you both have a variety of pets, split up your date so you have equal amounts of time getting to know each pet.
- ★ Bring a gift for the pet you're about to meet as a way to break the ice and make a good impression.
- ★ If your date's pet does not like you (or vice versa), then be safe, exercise caution, and set up boundaries so your relationship with your date doesn't get complicated alongside this other important relationship. Create a safe, separate living space for the pet until they get more comfortable.

LEVEL UP

During the date, take some pictures of your date having fun with their pet. Send the pics to them with a note or text describing what you appreciated about the date, even if it didn't go completely smoothly.

Talking Points

- Are you a pet lover? Have you always been or is it a new love?
- What is the best pet you've ever had?
- What's one pet you would never consider having?
- Are there any pets you can picture you and your date both caring for in the future?
- If you did not like your date's pet (or your date's pet does not like you), how will this affect your relationship moving forward?

PRANKSTERS

A cheerful heart is good medicine, but a broken spirit saps a person's strength.

—Proverbs 17:22

This date is pretty risky and daring to do with a close friend or couple you both know well, so choose someone who is lighthearted and enjoys a good laugh. Together with your date, plan a harmless and inoffensive prank on that friend. Although there are plenty of ideas online (from a simple conversation twist that confuses your friend to the good old-fashioned whoopie cushion that you slip onto their seat as they attempt to sit down), the overall goal is to create a joke with your date that you can play on a mutual friend.

What's the Word?

sometimes a good laugh is the best medicine. Although you may have great and laughable moments with your date, extending that joy to a friend through a good joke can be just as fun. If you know someone who could use a dose of that medicine, consider offering it together to express your shared love for that person. Telling a joke can evoke a great smile. Sharing a funny story can produce laughter for a day. Creating an entire experience that makes a cheerful memory can last a lifetime.

Good For

- Playfulness
- Friendship
- Teamwork

Tip

- Keep the prank wholesome. Some good examples include carefully replacing any pictures in frames with photos of you and your date. Another example is to offer them a bowl of M&M's, but fill the container with Skittles and Reese's Pieces instead.
- Do not prank or joke about realistic matters (like saying that someone is hurt, pregnant, breaking up, or cheating). These kinds of pranks can rub the wrong way, and that is not the intent of this date.
- Be sure the person (or couple) you choose will be open to the prank.
- Be careful with this date. It could start a prank war with you and your date (which can also be fun!).
- Remember, timing is everything.

LEVEL UP

While plotting out the prank for your friends, prank your date in the process.

Talking Points

- In what ways do you seek laughter in your life?
- How can you and your date laugh more in your relationship?
- What blessings do you currently have that give you a cheerful heart?

AMUSE YOURSELF

This is the day the Lord has made. We will rejoice and be glad in it.

—Psalm 118:24

Set up a group date for you, your date, and your closest friends to go to an amusement park, a carnival, a miniature golf course, or another fun destination. Maybe there is a place you and your friends went when you were younger. Or perhaps there is a place that you, your date, and your friends all wanted to visit but you just never found the opportunity. Choose your destination and round up the troops.

What's the Word?

God made each day for us to be glad, not for us to feel dreadful or worry how things will turn out. It's very important that you date someone who chooses to stay grateful, joyful, and present in the moments God has given you on a particular day. The same can be said about who you choose to establish friendships with. As you look around and see who is surrounding you, with gladness in your hearts remember there is plenty for you to rejoice about.

Good For

- Playfulness
- Friendship
- Being present

Tip

- Get tickets in advance (if necessary) and agree to meet friends at the entrance so you can simply walk in and begin to have fun.
- Although you may want to sit next to your date throughout the day, it's okay to sit with other friends instead. When playing games, mix it up and try couples vs. couples or boys vs. girls. When everyone engages with everyone, the fun is multiplied!
- This date might turn into a long day. Be prepared with water, snacks, and a charged phone, and wear proper attire, like comfortable shoes or a light jacket.
- You can still be flirty or romantic in this group setting. Hold hands, win your date a prize, or share some tasty treats together.
- It's better to keep the group outing to three or four couples. Doing so will maintain the group dynamic and limit your desire to want to split up and go separate ways.

LEVEL UP

While you're at an amusement park or carnival, steal a few private minutes together by going on a ride that can seat only two people, such as a Ferris wheel.

Talking Points

- What's the most fun thing you did on this date?
- What are you doing each day to rejoice, feel happy, and be glad?
- What can you do in your relationship to bring joy into each day?

MYSTERY DINNER

Ask me and I will tell you remarkable secrets you do not know about things to come.

—Jeremiah 33:3

Round up your date and 8 to 10 of your favorite friends, family members, or coworkers. With your date, plan out a murder mystery dinner at home. In most murder mystery cases, there is a murder scene and several clues, and everyone is a suspect. Create a murder story that involves a weapon, a location, and a reason the murder occurred. Then share the story and the clues throughout the dinner while your company tries to solve the case. If you're not sure where to start, simply look up "murder mystery dinner" online. You can review a range of options, from free PDFs of games you can host to elaborate boxed games that play out like a fun board game night. They can include invitations, character descriptions, props, and more!

What's the Word?

There's nothing like a great whodunit to build excitement and create tension in a room. Not knowing the full story and having to crack a case is enticing and, well, fun—when it's a game. In real life, having to discover the truths about and answers to our "why" and "how" questions can be stressful, not to mention facing all the mysteries that lie within your relationship. Will it last? Will you be happy? How will it all turn out? But with God, it's quite the opposite. He wants to reveal the answers. Through prayer, ask God your most mysterious questions and discover what He has to say.

Good For

- Teamwork
- Trust
- Playfulness

Tip

- Don't rush to end the date simply because the mystery was solved. Hang out afterward and offer dessert and coffee.
- Get into character the moment the date begins and encourage everyone else to do the same.
- Use your mystery dinner date character names as secret nicknames for each other that you can use throughout your relationship.
- The mystery is the primary reason for the dinner date, so be sure to make an easy meal. You don't want to worry over a cooking complication. There's nothing wrong with takeout, either!

- Remember, it's only a game. People will be pointing fingers and creating alliances, and will say anything to try to win the game. These actions can inadvertently stir up real feelings or be triggering for some who get easily offended. Whatever you do, aim to keep the date lighthearted and fun.

LEVEL UP

You can combine this date with "Netflix and Grill" for a murder-mystery themed couples' day or weekend.

Talking Points

- What was the most fun part of solving the murder mystery?
- Do you feel as though there are any mysteries in your relationship right now? If so, what?
- Share a situation where God revealed a mystery to you after you prayed about it.
- How often do you go to God to discover your life's mysteries?

GO FOR THE GOLD

Don't you realize that in a race everyone runs, but only one person gets the prize? So run to win!

—1 Corinthians 9:24

Create a day that is filled with fun and silly Olympic-style games so you and your date can compete against other two-person teams. Record your wins, and at the end of your date, have a ceremony for the teams who have won the most. Reward the top three teams with gold, silver, and bronze medals.

What's the Word?

God is well aware of how competitive humans are in nature. He's aware of the stakes, the training involved, and the emotional flood that comes whenever you are set to compete for the gold. Just as God offers you something much more valuable than a gold medal, your relationship offers you something of value as well: stability, companionship, and love. Like an athlete who gives his sport his whole heart, you must be willing to receive God's ultimate prize and win that "golden" relationship you long to have with your date.

Good For

- Encouraging each other
- Teamwork
- Support

Tip

- Search online for "Olympic games party" to find some great (and pretty hilarious) games fit for everyone! You might hold a potato sack race, balance a book on your head and race to a finish line, have an egg toss, or try to move an Oreo cookie from your forehead to your mouth without using your hands.
- Have each two-person team create a country name and flag to sport throughout the entire Olympic date!
- The best part of competing is receiving the medal. You can buy medals for this occasion or create gold, silver, and bronze candies, trophies, or handmade crafts.
- Some games may require you to have game props like plates and cups. Get all your game supplies in advance and set them up at each game station before everyone arrives.

- Your Olympic games don't have to be physical. Create games that challenge the mind (like Bible trivia), stage a pie-eating contest, or do something that requires one teammate to be blindfolded! Mix it up and make it enjoyable for everyone involved.

LEVEL UP

Create a special gold medal that you give your date after everyone leaves. Let them know how they have earned it within your relationship.

Talking Points

- Are you competitive at heart? Why or why not?
- Did you work well with your teammate? What could you have done better?
- In what ways are you aiming to have a relationship worth the gold?
- How are you running to win for God's kingdom in your everyday life?

KICK IT WITH THE KIDS

Children are a gift from the Lord; they are a reward from Him. Children born to a young man are like arrows in a warrior's hands.

—Psalm 127:3–4

This date is only for couples who have blended families. If you're eager to experience the joys of being with children together, check out "The Babysitter's Club". But blending families can be one of the most challenging things a new couple can go through, so this group date is designed to help them. On this date, you won't be enjoying time alone; instead, bring the kids along! Create a date that will entertain the children and allow you both to spend quality time with everyone. You could visit a local playground and follow that excursion with a picnic lunch, or go see a movie together before going to a restaurant the kids like.

What's the Word?

Children are blessings. A major part of your partner's life is their kids (or vice versa). A life without them simply does not (and will not!) exist. But kids should not be considered baggage. They are not meant to be roadblocks in the way of you drawing closer to your date. Children are blessings and rewards that enhance your (and your date's) legacy. How you treat them—and, more important, how you show love to them—will guide not just your relationship but also the blessings you receive from it.

Good For

★ Vulnerability
★Commitment★
Boundaries

Tip

- ★ Remember, this is still a date—do not make it all about the kids. Engage together with everyone.
- ★ Your kids or your date's kids might feel uncomfortable getting to know someone new. Take your time, respect their needs, and do not rush this process.

- You and your date might feel nervous about introducing your kids for the first time (if they haven't met before). Be sure that you, your date, and the kids are ready to take this step. Do not rush it. If the season is not right, hold off until it is.
- Older kids may need to be entertained differently than younger kids. As long as you are able to spend some devoted time with them and allow them to be themselves, you can still have a successful date and establish a real connection.
- Pay attention to how your date responds to meeting the kids in your life (and vice versa). It's a big step, and their focus is most likely on their own kids. So take it slow and go at a pace that is comfortable for them.

LEVEL UP

Bring gifts for everyone on the date, like flowers, chocolates, or anything else you think your date and the kids will enjoy.

Talking Points

- What was it like to have a date with the kids?
- What were your concerns about the kids meeting you or your date?
- What do you think a blended family looks and feels like?
- How does having kids remind you that they are God's blessings, rewards, and arrows in the hands of a warrior?

DATE MY PARENTS

Honor your father and mother. Then you will live a long, full life in the land the Lord your God is giving you.

—Exodus 20:12

Parents are a big deal. They have known you longest and they helped raise you to be the person you are today. Go on a date with your date's parents. Take their mom to lunch or spend time outdoors with their dad. Create the opportunity to get a one-on-one experience with them as a way to draw closer to your date. If you or your date no longer have parents in your life, you can always spend time with an older family member you're still close to. Or if you have older children who are of dating age, you can suggest this date as an idea to get to know their significant others.

What's the Word?

Honoring your parents can be challenging no matter what your relationship is like. By inviting them into your relationship and sharing them with someone you care about, you open the doors for them to understand your relationship and get to know better someone who is meaningful to you. It may not come easy, but it's worth working toward. Looking at it from the other side, by reaching beyond your own relationship with your partner and cultivating a relationship with their parents as an extension of them, you're honoring your relationship. By inviting parental figures into this part of your life and heart, you are showing them exactly how much they mean to you now and in future seasons.

Good For

- Vulnerability
- Commitment
- Honoring values

Tip

- Respect parents at all times. They might be just as nervous as you are about making the right impression.
- Be yourself when meeting your date's parents. Show them why the two of you are together in the first place.
- Go with the flow. Step out of your comfort zone a bit and be open to different types of family activities and eating unfamiliar foods.
- Don't be afraid to talk about love, relationships, and your date—they might have buckets of wisdom on the subject matter.
- Parents care deeply for their children, and are especially concerned about their children's partners. Your job is to let them know that their child is in good hands.

LEVEL UP

Make a list of things you appreciate about your date and share it with their parents or family. Let them know you value the relationship you have been blessed with.

Talking Points

- What was it like to date your date's parents?
- In what ways did you bond with your date's parents?
- What did you learn about your date from their parents?
- How do you feel your parents made you who you are today, in both positive and negative ways?

CHAPTER SEVEN

Holidays & Special Occasions

Although dates can be sporadic and spontaneous, sometimes you need to think of ways to connect during the special times of the year, every year. This chapter is all about using the calendar to find inspiration for memorable dates. Holidays and special occasions can often be seen as a dating challenge, mainly because there is so much tradition involved with these events. Maybe every Christmas is celebrated at Grandma's house. Or on Thanksgiving, you always follow the same menu. On certain holidays, family may be expected to come first and your significant other second.

Tradition is a value I cherish. At the same time, I value the idea of creating and establishing new traditions. The dates within this chapter will allow you to create your own holiday traditions while continuing to keep the old ones. Setting new things in place can not only help you learn to love each other better but also give your holiday season a fresh makeover and create a totally new approach to your season. These dates may be the boost you need to cherish the old, appreciate the new, and give you and your date something to look forward to every year.

THE SWEETEST CHRISTMAS GIFT

How sweet your words taste to me; they are sweeter than honey.

—Psalm 119:103

'Tis the season of giving! During this Christmas season, you and are your date are going to work together to create small Christmas packages of cookies filled with scriptures, prayers, and words of good cheer for the people you love. Pick a day when you and your date can work together in the kitchen to bake, decorate, and pack your sweet gifts to distribute.

What's the Word?

Baking cookies is a big holiday activity. It's fun to do together, and it creates an opportunity to pass out a sweet touch of love to those you care about. Sweeter than what you bake is what God says. The Bible lets us know that His words are sweeter than honey. And when you choose to share His words with those you love, the aftertaste and satisfaction will linger much longer.

Good For

- Compassion
- Teamwork
- Support

Tip

- Do not get overwhelmed by this date. Choose between one and four cookie recipes you both would like to try. Work together, one recipe at a time, or split up the recipes so you're both doing an equal amount of work to create your tasty treats.
- Make the baking fun and interesting by mixing things up, such as making vegan cookies, adding fruits or nuts, decorating one batch with icing, and sprinkling coffee grounds into the batter.
- Think of special ways to dress up your cookie packages. Use jars, tin containers, boxes, ribbon, and special wrapping.
- Encourage your date as they bake. Not everyone is a great cook, but the point is to spread love around together. No matter how the cookies turn out, your words will keep your date uplifted.
- Put on some Christmas music to get you into the holiday spirit and set the tone for the date.

LEVEL UP

Make a special batch of cookies in honor of your date. Pick something they'll love that incorporates their favorite ingredients.

Talking Points

- which cookie is your favorite? why?
- If you don't usually love baking, was it more fun to do the activity with your date? Was it more challenging?
- How does it feel to receive something homemade as a gift?
- What was the best part of working together?
- when working together, what's the best way your date can encourage you?
- which Bible verse always lifted you up and inspired you?

DANCING LIGHTS

The light shines in the darkness, and the darkness can never extinguish it.

—John 1:5

On the Fourth of July, fireworks race to the sky, exploding in color that lights up the darkness—a romantic symbol of freedom for all. How about making this concept personal? On this date, when the night is dark, warm, and calm, light two flying paper lanterns in honor of your relationship. Then release them into the sky as symbols of the light you can bring to the world together.

What's the Word?

God is the ultimate light shining in our lives. As long as we set our sights on Him, rather than the darkness that may surround us, we will always find hope rising, freedom dancing, and love enduring. The light of God's love never burns out. You can demonstrate that same love in your relationship, giving you the same results. Although we are not God, we do have access to His love, and we can learn to shine that love on others in any circumstance. If you're looking to let your relationship rise without limits, you must allow God's love to shine in you through all trials, all circumstances, and all endeavors.

Good For

* Intimacy
* Affection
* Unconditional love

Tip

* Paper lanterns are made of paper, naturally. Write words of affection, devotion, commitment, and prayers for your date directly onto the lantern. Before lighting them into the sky, read them to each other.
* Be careful where you light your lantern. Make sure you do so away from telephone poles, trees, and the like.
* Bring a flashlight so you can see your lantern soaring high in the sky.
* Play some romantic music to dance to as you watch your lanterns fly away.
* Remember, always exercise caution when dealing with fire.

LEVEL UP

Increase your light by attending a lantern festival where many other participants light lanterns together to create a magical scene.

Talking Points

- In what ways are you looking to God's light during life's dark moments?
- How does your date light up your life?
- What are you doing to be a consistent light to the people in your lives?

PLUS ONE

Then the Lord God said, "It is not good for the man to be alone. I will make a helper who is just right for him."

—Genesis 2:18

There is always a season for a wedding. When you're invited to attend one, you're usually allowed to bring a guest. Although this date may seem a bit intense for a new relationship, it doesn't have to create pressure in yours! Just be excited for those who are getting married and celebrate with them. No matter what your situation is, you can observe the blessing of God bringing two people together. And don't forget to have fun! Dance with your date and enjoy the day.

What's the Word?

Marriage was a part of God's original plan. He made us to come together in love, to fulfill His plans and purpose. On this date, you and your date will witness two people come together for the first time in holy matrimony. Are you and your partner looking toward marriage, or are you still in the early stages of your relationship? Perhaps you have been married for years and can recall exactly what those feelings were like when you stood at the altar. Maybe you've been married before and aren't eager to rush back. Wherever life and this relationship have taken you, remember why God invented marriage in the first place: to share His love with others.

Good For

- Commitment
- Communication
- Being present

Tip

- Just for fun, wear an outfit that complements your date's, such as the same color scheme or a similar pattern.
- Dance, eat, have fun, and do not be shy or embarrassed. It's a celebration, after all. Create more fun with your date by making a bingo card and filling in the spots with your wedding predictions (like guessing the cake flavor, what songs the DJ will play, or how long the best man's speech will be), then play the game together as you enjoy the wedding.
- People may be asking about your relationship, so know where you're at together before you answer anyone else.
- If you're married already, whisper the vows to each other as a discreet way to be romantic.

- If you're not married yet but you may be headed in that direction, use this date as an opportunity to consider what would and wouldn't work for you. Observe the ways the ceremony and reception reflect the bride and groom's values as a couple.

LEVEL UP

At the end of this date, pray together about future steps in your relationship. Share in your prayer your desires, fears, and intentions, and ask God to show both of you the way to the future He wants for you. Ask for God's blessings for the happy couple, too, and say a prayer for them every year on their anniversary.

Talking Points

- For nonmarried: What does your dream wedding look like?
- For married: Did anything stand out in this particular wedding that reminded you of your own?
- How did it feel to attend a wedding with your date?
- Did any parts of this date make you feel uncomfortable? If so, what were they?
- What does "a helper in marriage" look like to you?
- Did this wedding bring up any thoughts regarding your own relationship?

GOTTA LOVE CHOCOLATE

Dear friends, let us continue to love one another, for love comes from God. Anyone who loves is a child of God and knows God.

—1 John 4:7

People often give chocolate on Valentine's Day as a sign and symbol of love. On this date, in honor of Valentine's Day, make your own box of chocolates for your date. Together, melt chocolate chips into candy-making molds, add extra ingredients, and sprinkle a bit of your love into your recipes. Don't forget to stash your treats in a box for your Valentine to enjoy.

What's the Word?

How could something as simple as chocolate be used to express love? It's in the way it tastes. It's in how it makes you feel. It's rich. It's divine. And it leaves you wanting more. Now think about the real nature of love: God is love. Love is God. These are simple yet very profound statements. If such wonderful things can be said about chocolate, just imagine how the love of God can make you feel. Consider what His love means to you. If you have just a tiny dose of that love reflected in your relationship, consider yourself blessed and standing in the very presence of God.

Good For

- Intimacy
- Affection
- Unconditional love

Tip

- You can select any candy-making mold you like. It can be as basic as a simple candy bar shape, or shaped like a heart, a rose, or a teddy bear to honor the Valentine's Day theme. You can even choose a silly mold that reflects a shared interest, like an animal shape or a Star Wars theme.

- Set a romantic ambiance for your date using music, flowers, and candles.
- To kick up the intimacy a notch, if your date is comfortable, feed your chocolates to each other.
- For every piece of chocolate you make, tell your date one thing you like or appreciate about them.

LEVEL UP

Use a very special keepsake box (either purchased or handmade) to store your date's chocolates so they can cherish this date long after the chocolates are gone.

Talking Points

- Are you a chocolate person? What do you love most about chocolate?
- Does chocolate symbolize love or romance for you? If not, what does?
- At what point in your relationship did you realize you loved your date (if you've reached this point already)?
- How does the love you have for your date reflect the love God has for you?

MUFFINS, MACY'S, AND A MOMENT TOGETHER

I always thank my God when I pray for you.

—Philemon 4:1

Thanksgiving is a time to come together with family and close friends to express gratitude. It's a loving and touching holiday that is often full of family traditions, and the day itself can get pretty jam-packed. On this date, before the hustle and bustle of the holiday festivities begin, share a simple breakfast with your date. This date is meant to give you some one-on-one time with each other that you might not get during the rest of the day.

What's the Word?

There is much to be thankful for, but you cannot always express it in the way you would like. This day may be filled with gratitude for everything and everyone else, especially if you have a large family or friend group, and you may not be focusing on your romantic relationship. Take a moment in the morning to express gratitude for this special person. After all you both have been through, whether you're a new couple or long married, don't skip cherishing this morning moment. Knowing you took the time out to share your thankfulness with each other will make the rest of the day that much better.

Good For

- Intimacy
- Being present
- Affection
- Compassion

Tip

- Keep it simple to avoid overwhelming feelings or a time crunch. Either bake muffins the night before or purchase something special for breakfast.

- Re-create a fun childhood memory together by watching the Macy's Thanksgiving Day Parade. If it isn't your cup of tea, you and your date can always enjoy a morning walk or casual conversation instead.
- Be sure that during this breakfast date you express your gratitude for your date and your relationship.
- Before leaving, pray over each other and for all the things and people you are thankful for.
- Turn off your devices. Try to disconnect from the rest of the world during this morning moment with your date, and aim to share this time with no one but them.

LEVEL UP

If you aren't so pressed for time or if you don't plan on indulging later, turn your muffin breakfast into a mini Thanksgiving feast with pumpkin spice lattes, turkey bacon, sweet potato hash, and other Thanksgiving-themed breakfast items.

Talking Points

- Name five things you are thankful for this year.
- What are you most thankful for when it comes to your relationship?
- In what ways can you express your thankfulness for your date throughout the year?
- In what ways can you express your thankfulness for God each day?

BELLS AND KETTLES

Blessed are those who are generous, because they feed the poor.

—Proverbs 22:9

Each holiday season, you see and hear the same thing outside stores and restaurants: a tiny bell ringing with the sight of a shiny red kettle. It's the charity campaign for the Salvation Army that dates back to 1891 in efforts to feed the poor across the world during the holiday season. On this date, you and your partner will volunteer for a day to ring the bell in your area to collect donations for this cause.

What's the Word?

How often have you gone past the bell and red kettle? How often have you supported them through your giving? So often, your life is so full of blessings you don't think twice about it. Yet with each generous act, you will be blessed in return. When you act as a couple to willingly go into your community to seek generosity from others, your relationship will be blessed as a result.

Good For

★ Compassion ★ Being present ★ Vulnerability

Tip

- ★ Sign up to volunteer for this service by going to the Salvation Army's site: RegisterToRing.com.
- ★ Dress appropriately for this date. It will be in the winter season, you will be standing for long periods, and you will most likely be outside.

- Take turns ringing the bell. Serve your date by bringing them a cup of coffee or hot chocolate during your time together.
- You may not get donations. Don't attach your personal feelings to what you get. Remember, you're extending this opportunity for others to give. Your own giving is in sacrificing your time to ring the bell and collect.
- If this service is not offered in your area, you can always create your own giving bucket. Use a bell to draw attention and donate your proceeds to your local food drive. (You may need to get authorization from that organization first.)

LEVEL UP

Your date might get chilly during this date, so present them with a cozy scarf or gloves they can wear throughout this date and the rest of the season.

Talking Points

- How did it feel to stand in front of strangers and ring a bell to ask for donations?
- What was it like when you received donations? What was it like when no one donated?
- In what ways are you generous in your everyday living?
- How can you and your date be generous throughout the year?

NEW YEAR'S BUCKET LIST

So let's not get tired of doing what is good. At just the right time we will reap a harvest of blessing if we don't give up.

—Galatians 6:9

It's the last day of the year, and although you and your date may already have plans to spend the evening ringing in the new one, you still have the day to do something great. Do you have a relationship goal you never got around to doing this year? That one destination? That one project? That one conversation? Today is the day! Before the clock strikes midnight, you and your date are challenged to make it happen while there's still time left.

What's the Word?

Time is still on your side. As long as you have time, the opportunity to do something is not lost. You can still accomplish the goals you have for your life and for this relationship. More important, do not give up on what God is aiming to do within your life and your relationship. Enter the new year together knowing you've accomplished a lot, grown a lot, and continued to sow seeds together. From there, your relationship will most certainly flourish.

Good For

- Trust
- Being present
- Support

Tip

- Don't overwhelm yourself with this date. Keep it realistic. If you're not able to run the 5K you missed this year, go for a light jog with your date instead.
- On this date, the more spontaneous gestures, the better, so improvise, go with the flow, and have fun.

- Depending on what's on your bucket list (and how daring you and your date are) you may need some time in advance to plan this out.
- Take note of how you and your date handle time-sensitive situations. Also, observe how you and your date support each other in these circumstances.
- At the end of the day, it's not the end of the world, only the end of a year. Tomorrow is a new day. If there's something you just weren't able to do this year despite your best efforts, give it another chance in the new year.

LEVEL UP

Create a bucket list together for the new year.

Talking Points

- Why did you feel you needed to do this thing before the year ended?
- What kept you from doing this thing in the first place?
- Is there anything God is telling you not to give up on?
- In times of weariness, how can your date help you not to quit? How can you help your date?

SUPER BIG BIRTHDAY BASH BONANZA

May He grant your heart's desires and make all your plans succeed.

—Psalm 20:4

This birthday celebration is a bit tricky because there are many layers to it. But if you execute it properly, it will be a birthday to remember! On your date's birthday, set up a day when you can do their favorite things. But each time your date transitions to a new thing (e.g., dinner is over, then you head to the movies), you must surprise them with a new birthday gift before the next part of the day.

What's the Word?

God wants to give you the desires of your heart. He wants to because He loves you. He wants to see you succeed, be happy, and live a joyous life. What would having the desires of your heart look like for you on a daily basis? Although you may not get to experience a birthday bonanza every day, God is moving to bless you with the desires of your heart all the time. That means every single day of your life God doing something that will help make all your plans succeed, as long as they are aligned with His plans. Trust Him in all things. Trust Him when it comes to the desires you have for this relationship. Trust is the key to unlocking those plans and living a life where every day can feel like a birthday!

Good For

- Affection
- Unconditional love
- Support

Tip

- Infuse your date's love language into every portion of this date. Every gift, surprise, place, and activity must incorporate their love language. You can discover what their love language is by using the online resource found in the Resources section.

- Don't feel pressure to give an expensive gift with every transition. A small but meaningful token, a sweet letter, or a homemade item are great options.
- Try to make sure your date doesn't know what's coming. You have to be one step ahead at all times. You may need to plan out this celebration weeks (or even months) in advance.
- If you don't know the desires of your date's heart, ask! Ideally, you should bring it up very casually in conversation at least a month in advance so they don't suspect anything.
- Create shock value with this date by adding some completely unexpected gifts, activities, or gestures.

LEVEL UP

Get your date's family and friends involved by planning a grand finale surprise party or weekend getaway.

Talking Points

- How did it feel to create this birthday event for your date?
- How did your date react to each new item or activity as the date went on?
- What are your desires for this relationship?
- What are the desires of your heart?
- How does it make you feel to know that God wants to give you the desires of your heart?

Made in the USA
Monee, IL
08 July 2024